DERBYSHIRE
FIGHTER ACES
OF WORLD WAR TWO

DERBYSHIRE
FIGHTER ACES
OF WORLD WAR TWO

BARRY M. MARSDEN

TEMPUS

Dedicated to the Derbyshire 'Few', and in particular to those fighter aces who received no official recognition for their gallant and meritorious service in the defence of freedom.

Front cover: On 14 August 1940, Alan Feary of 609 Squadron pursued a Ju 88 which had just bombed the base at Middle Wallop. This painting shows him chasing the enemy raider over Boscombe Down, where he sent it crashing to destruction. (B. Norman)

First published 2004

Tempus Publishing Limited
The Mill, Brimscombe Port,
Stroud, Gloucestershire, GL5 2QG
www.tempus-publishing.com

British Library Cataloguing in Publication Data.
A catalogue record for this book is available from the British Library.

ISBN 0 7524 3173 0

Typesetting and origination by Tempus Publishing Limited.
Printed in Great Britain by Midway Colour Print, Wiltshire.

Contents

Acknowledgements

In preparing this book, I would like to thank the following for their great help in providing information and photographs relating to the fighter aces whose combat careers form the basis of the work. Without their assistance, it would have remained an unrealised ambition.

Harry Baker; Tony Bartley; John Bisdee; Henry Boot; Michael F.J. Bowyer; Peter Cornwell; David Drake-Feary; John Flinders; John Foreman; Norman Fryer; Chris Goss; Marjorie Hancock; Sydney Hanson; Donald Higgins; Ray Holmes; Mike Hopkins; Trudi Humberstone; Jeanne Jackson; the *Kent Messenger*; Simon Parry; Sallie Ratledge; David Roberts; Bill Rolls; Philip Sanders; Andrew Saunders; Chris Shores; Pauline Sturdy; Johnathan Woolley.

Photographs

Whilst every effort has been made to acknowledge the sources of the illustrations used in this work, the origins of some of the pictures are varied and often obscure. Some originate from private collections, whilst others come from organisations and agencies no longer in existence. The publication of photographs whose derivation is doubtful is unintentional, but it is hoped that their appearance in this book will be seen as a fitting tribute to the Derbyshire fighter aces who participated in the Second World War.

Introduction

They shall mount up with wings, as eagles
Isaiah 40: 31

As an author long interested in military aviation, I have developed a particular affinity for the fighter aircraft and tactics of Second World War, and as a Derbyshireman have been drawn to the combat careers of the fighter aces born and bred within my home county. Encouraged by the successful production of a little work entitled *A Few of the Derbyshire 'Few'*, which was published in 1987 and quickly sold out, and the setting-up of a permanent memorial to the Derby Battle of Britain ace Sergeant Pilot Alan Feary in the city's Industrial Museum, I decided to delve more deeply into the subject of Derbyshire's fighter pilots of the 1939-1945 period. I am well aware that equally worthy histories could be compiled of the county's Bomber and other Command flyers, but leave that task to other hands. As a result of my research, I have uncovered a wealth of material which has been synthesized into a series of diverse narratives describing the war service of a number of gallant young men, some of whom paid the full sacrifice in the fight against Fascism.

Derbyshire fighter pilots fought from the first to the last day of the Second World War. They were present over France in the Phoney War, and during the German *Blitzkreig* on the West. They made their mark in the Battle of Britain, flew over occupied Europe in 1941, and operated in Syria, the Western Desert and over Malta, Sicily, Italy and Greece. One was even involuntarily involved in the hunt for the German battleship, *Bismarck*! They combated Focke-Wulf Condors over the Atlantic and the Japanese over the Timor Sea. Derbyshire men flew sweeps, escorts and fighter-bomber missions before and after D-Day, and attended the final death throes of the Luftwaffe in the last months of the conflict. They knew bad times and good, and made their contribution world-wide to the inevitable and final defeat of the Axis.

It is gratifying to record that the survivors and their families and friends were only too glad to help recall and proudly perpetuate their vital achievements. The result has been a labour of love, and my sole personal regret was in noting how unevenly distributed their awards for gallantry were. Several aces who deserved decorations for their outstanding service were shamefully neglected, and a glance over their stories will quickly establish their right to the honours they merited, but were all too frequently denied. I sincerely hope that this belated tribute will ensure that the sacrifices of Derbyshire's worthy airborne heroes are not entirely lost to mind.

The table on the following page records the victories of all Derbyshire pilots who flew single-seat fighters, and the first ten of these are profiled in this book.

Barry M. Marsden
Eldwick
January 2004

Provisional List of Victories Claimed by Derbyshire Pilots Flying Single-Seat Fighters

Pilot	Shared	Destroyed	Probable	Damaged
Sqn Ldr A.V. Clowes	8	–	3	2
Flt Lt N. Taylor	8	2	1	3
Air Cdre P.J. Sanders	6	–	2	1
Sgt A.N. Feary	5	1	1	5
Sqn Ldr J.L. Flinders	5	1	–	1
Sqn Ldr H.C. Baker	4	2	–	5
Sgt W.B. Higgins	4	1	–	1
Sqn Ldr N.V. Glew	3	3	2	7
PO F. Mellor	2	3	1	3
Wg Cdr F.G. Woolley	4	–	1	1
PO F.R. Walker-Smith	3	1	–	–
Flt Lt J.E. Van Shaick	2	–	1	3
Flt Lt C.E.Bowen	2	1	–	3
PO D.C. Shepley	2	–	–	–
Flt Lt J.S. Anderson	1	2	–	1
Sqn Ldr L.F. Henstock	–	3	1	3
PO W.L. Davis	1	–	1	1
PO J.A. Wain	1	–	–	3
Flt Lt F. Meakin	–	1	–	–
PO C.W.J. Fearn	–	–	–	2
TOTAL	**61**	**24**	**14**	**45**

The ranks listed are the highest attained during the pilots' service careers.

one

Squadron Leader
Arthur Victor Clowes
DFC DFM

Combat Record

Date	Sqn	Locality	Aircraft Flown	Enemy Type	Claim
23.11.39	1	N.E. Saarbrücken	Hurricane I L1842 JX–T	Heinkel III	Destroyed
29.03.40	1	Bouzanville	Hurricane I L1969	Messerschmitt 110	Destroyed (shared)
14.05.40	1	Sedan Le Chesne	Hurricane I	Messerschmitt 109E Junkers 87B	Destroyed Destroyed
15.05.40	1	Vouziers	Hurricane I	Messerschmitt 110C	Destroyed
23.05.40	1	Rouen	Hurricane I	Heinkel III	Destroyed (shared)
14.06.40	1	Evreux	Hurricane I	Messerschmitt 109E Messerschmitt 109E	Destroyed Damaged
16.08.40	1	Guildford Petworth	Hurricane I P3169 JX–T	Heinkel IIIP Heinkel IIIP	Destroyed Destroyed
30.08.40	1	Epping	Hurricane I P3395 JX–B	Heinkel III Heinkel III Messerschmitt 110C	Damaged Damaged Damaged
31.08.40	1	Chelmsford Martlesham	Hurricane I P9935 JX–B	Dornier 17Z Dornier 17Z Messerschmitt 110C	Probable Probable Probable
07.09.40	1	Thames Estuary	Hurricane I P9935 JX–B	Messerschmitt 110C	Destroyed
24.10.40	1	Eaton Socon	Hurricane I P9935 JX–B	Dornier 215B	Destroyed (shared)

Squadron Leader Arthur Victor Clowes DFC DFM

ARTHUR VICTOR CLOWES was the most celebrated fighter pilot produced by Derbyshire in the Second World War. He is credited with the destruction of up to twelve enemy aircraft, and served with distinction throughout the conflict.

His Derbyshire origins have been obscured by writers who have insisted on regarding him as a Welshman nicknamed 'Taffy'; a mistake presumably resulting initially from Shores' and Williams' *Aces High,* published in 1966, and repeated in subsequent works. However, unless the Principality has secretly annexed his native shire, 'Darky' Clowes' birthplace can be confidently fixed as the village of New Sawley, which is close to the River Trent in south Derbyshire, where he was born on 12 August 1912. Arthur's only connection with Wales was through his Welsh-born wife, whom he married in the spring of 1940.

Arthur was brought up by his grandparents, his father having been killed in the First World War. Arthur Victor Clowes Senior, a private in the 1st/5th Battalion Sherwood Foresters (Notts and Derby), was killed on 1 July 1917 and has no known grave. He is commemorated on the Arras Memorial in the Pas de Calais. His niece told me that his mother subsequently became involved with an Australian soldier with whom she disappeared to the Antipodes, to be heard of no more! His only other close relative was his sister Gertrude (Trudi), four years his senior, who recently died in Canada, where his relatives now reside. He attended Tamworth Road School, Long Eaton, and from an early age seems to have been set on a career in the Royal Air Force. On 15 January 1929, at the age of sixteen, he enlisted as 563046 Aircraft Apprentice A.V. Clowes, serving with the No.4 Wing, Halton. He trained as a rigger, and during the early 1930s gradually climbed the promotional ladder, remustering as a fitter in early 1936. Later that year he was considered suitable for pilot training and joined No.6 Flying Training School, first soloing in an Avro Tutor biplane in September.

A female friend who knew him well during this time has a clear and abiding memory of Arthur, then a dark-haired, saturnine (hence the 'Darky' nickname) and extremely presentable young man whom she first met at a dance in Nottingham. By this time his sister had married and was living in the city. Arthur spent many of his leaves with her, and must have regarded the house at Sherwood as his new home. He is remembered as likeable, popular and an inveterate joker with a good sense of humour. On their first meeting he excused his attire – black long-sleeved jersey and slacks – by persuading her he was a night watchman, snatching time off from guarding a hole somewhere on the road to Leicester!

Arthur Clowes clearly had ambitions and, though a loner, was 'one of those people one never forgets'. He was certainly attractive, with an infectious, strong personality which 'upon entering, would set the room alight.' Parents, sisters and their friends looked forward to his regular visits with excited anticipation during those last, fragile months of peace. Darky drove a dilapidated Riley 9 soft-top called Bertha, with a sagging, leaking roof, in which, it is recalled, he made his way around somewhat erratically. Like many pilots, Arthur is remembered as being superstitious and he invariably carried his good luck charm: a small carved ivory Buddha. After successfully completing his flying training he was promoted to sergeant pilot, and posted to the prestigious No.1 Squadron at Tangmere, Sussex, in May 1937. No.1 Squadron flew the elegant Hawker Fury biplane; manoeuverable, small, and with a high rate of climb, Furies epitomised all that was best in Britain's pre-war Fighter Command.

Two other Derbyshire-born officer pilots served with No.1 during the period between 1937 and 1939: Philip Sanders from Chesterfield and Lawrie Henstock, who hailed from Ashbourne. Many subsequently famous pilots also flew with No.1 and Darky found himself in exalted company. He honed his flying skills alongside his distinguished companions, and a photograph from the Squadron Archives shows him posing with his colleagues and their camouflaged biplanes in the autumn of 1938, when it was fully expected that, should the Munich negotiations fail, the nation would be at war. Fortunately, soon afterwards, the first of the new monoplane interceptors, the Hawker Hurricane, was delivered, the unit re-equipping with the rugged eight-gun fighters over the winter. By March 1939

Left: *A photograph of Sergeant Pilot Arthur Victor Clowes, dating from the winter of 1939.*
(T. Humberstone) Right: *Airman 'Darky' Clowes, aged sixteen, poses proudly for this studio portrait taken on joining the RAF in January 1929.* (T. Humberstone)

all the pilots were checked out on the type, and Arthur is recorded as being 'well pleased' with the new mounts. The Hurricane, a lineal descendent of the Fury, handled very much like its predecessor, apart from the greatly increased speed. The only early difficulties concerned the fixed-pitch, two-blade wooden Watts airscrew, which could not absorb the full power of the Merlin engine, and icing problems with the eight wing-guns, which prevented their operation above 15,000 feet.

In April 1939 a new CO, Squadron Leader P.J.H. 'Bull' Halahan, arrived at Tangmere. The Irishman was to transform the unit with his drive and considerable presence, and he was responsible for a series of innovations which were to have great significance for the future success of No.1 Squadron. The first was inaugurated in May, when, at the risk of a court martial, he had the eight guns of the unit's Hurricanes harmonised to converge on their targets at 250 yards, in defiance of the rigidly-enforced 400 yard 'hosepipe' pattern insisted upon by Dowding, C-in-C, Fighter Command. Halahan's order was a direct result of the poor scores achieved by the squadron crack shots using the spread pattern at their air-firing exercises at Sutton Bridge. Halahan was without doubt a fine leader who treated the sergeant pilots under his command with respect – as fellow pilots – and not some inferior species, an attitude regrettably apparent in the way some NCO pilots were used in certain RAF units.

As war approached it was arranged that when the British Expeditionary Force was formed for service in France, No.1 would become part of a four-squadron group tasked with providing air cover for the Army. On 8 September, six days after the British declaration of war, twelve Hurricanes lifted off from Tangmere, heading for Octeville near Le Havre. After an evening booze-up spent in the many fleshpots of the port, the somewhat fragile pilots were set to work digging slit trenches, and then indulged in a spectacular beat-up of the city. Various movements followed before Darky's squadron along with 73, their sister unit, were formed into 67 Wing, the former based at Vassincourt, 50 miles east of Rheims on a hill near Bar-le-Duc.

Darky and his fellow pilots began devoting time to sector reconnaissance and familiarising themselves with the topography of the local landscape and the position of diversion airfields before carrying out their first operational patrols. While awaiting the expected attack on France, when they would escort Advanced Air Striking Force (AASF) bombing sorties, No.1 were to fly standing patrols along the Franco-German frontier between Nancy and Metz – the so-called 'Right Front' – in search of hostile reconnaissance aircraft, with 73 covering to the west.

The Bull's second contribution to his squadron's well-being was to order a modification to the under-surface colour of their Hurricanes. Whilst German aeroplanes had their undersides sensibly painted light blue, and were thus very hard to spot from beneath, RAF aircraft had their undersides painted a ludicrous half black, half white. This made them painfully visible from below, and whilst this was theoretically an aid to recognition by Allied ack-ack gunners, in practice 'friendly' anti-aircraft fire was often directed at No.1's Hurricanes in direct defiance of their colour scheme. Halahan realised it was only a matter of time before the gunners were lucky and had all the unit's fighters repainted duck-egg blue underneath, arguing the point later. In due course all British day fighters gave up the black/white scheme and settled for the same inconspicuous undershade as the enemy.

Sergeant Clowes first went into action on 23 November 1939, which was only the second time his squadron had engaged the Luftwaffe since their arrival in France. He doubtless wore the white flying overalls which became his trademark over the ensuing years. He was in the Blue 3 slot, 'B' Flight led by Flt Lt Plinston on the Nancy-Metz line at 22,000 feet in line-astern at around 11.45 a.m. Suddenly anti-aircraft shellbursts below directed the section towards the sinister dark-coloured shape of a Heinkel III of 2(F)/122, coded F6+FK, heading back to Germany. Plinston and his number two, 'Pussy' Palmer, led the attack, but only four of the leader's Brownings responded to the button, presumably due to gun-bay icing caused by the congealing of lubricating oil in the belt links. Plinston claimed black smoke was vomiting from the raider's port motor as he broke away, but Palmer's eight guns failed

Trainee pilot Clowes shown flying his first solo in an Avro Cadet in the autumn of 1936. (T. Humberstone)

completely and he veered off in frustration. Arthur, who was piloting L1842 JX-T dived down onto the enemy aircraft, firing a short burst in a quarter attack as he closed, then climbed and swooped down for a second run.

Suddenly the sky seemed full of humped-backed, radial-engined fighters as a flight of six French Curtiss Hawk H-75As of GC11/5 arrived in an attempt to pick off the bomber in front of No.1's noses. Clowes reported that 'the method adopted by the French was to attack from all angles'. Threading his way between the 'friendlies' he came into line-astern of his quarry, hanging on behind to deliver three long bursts, raking the Heinkel with the concentrated fire of his two close-set batteries of wing guns. There was some return fire from the dorsal gunner before the raider dipped its port wing. One crew member baled out at 6,000 feet before the plane plunged vertically, crashing in flames in a forest north-east of Saarbrücken.

As Darky shaped to break away, he felt a jolt as something smashed into the rear of his Hurricane. It was one of the Armée de l'Air Hawks, impatient to get in on the act, which had collided with him, shearing off one of his elevators and much of the rudder. Apparently the French pilot had to bale out after his misjudgement, and the Derbyshire flier, his fighter badly damaged by the impact, struggled back to base, where he had to land at around 120 miles an hour to maintain control. In the process L1842 overshot and tipped up on its nose, leaving its pilot unhurt but somewhat shaken. A fellow-pilot, Paul Richey, author of *Fighter Pilot*, recorded that Arthur 'put up a very good show in getting his machine back to the airfield. I saw him straight after this little effort, and though he was laughing, he was trembling violently and could not talk coherently.' Small wonder!

The credit for the He 111 should really go to Clowes alone. His section leader admitted that the sergeant 'finished the Heinkel off' by delivering the knockout punch after the malfunction of his colleague's armament. Clowes' combat report was amusingly couched in the stiff, formal phraseology of the time, beginning with 'Sir, I have the honour to report the destruction of one Heinkel IIIK' and

Darky shows off Bertha, his beloved Riley convertible, sometime in the late 1930s. (M. Hancock)

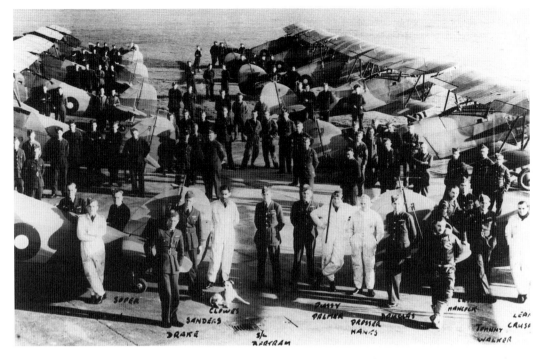

The No.1 squadron pilots and ground crew line up by their hastily-camouflaged Furies at Tangmere at the time of the Munich crisis. Darky, in customary white overalls, stands behind the squadron mascot, a hound of indeterminate ancestry. On his right is Philip Sanders, who was also serving with the unit at the time. (Squadron Archives)

concluding 'I have the honour to be, Sir, your obedient servant.' Future reports tended to be far more businesslike affairs as the tempo of battle increased.

As the result of another combat on the same day, the Bull made another contribution to the RAF's fighting efficiency. He purloined some back armour from a wrecked Fairey Battle light bomber and had it fixed behind the seat of one of his Hurricanes. Again, higher authority disapproved, insisting that the extra weight would upset the trim of the aeroplane. One of the squadron pilots flew the modified Hurricane to Farnborough and threw it around the skies over the airfield. This display convinced the doubters, and subsequently back armour was fitted throughout Fighter Command, saving the lives of many pilots.

No.1 Squadron had a quiet winter, training and patrolling whenever the weather allowed. Billy Drake, an officer pilot with the unit, later a 28 victory ace, became less than enamoured with the CO during this period. As he recalled in his book *Billy Drake, Fighter Leader*, published in 2002, Halahan 'seemed to have deserted us and moved into the much greater comfort of a nearby chateau. It was rumoured that he had fitted himself up not only with warm, comfortable accommodation, but also with some feminine company' – this despite the fact that the 'Bull' was a married man!

On the morning of 29 March 1940, one section of the squadron ran into Messerschmitt 109s – the first fighter-versus-fighter combat for the unit since 1918. Little had as yet been seen of Goering's new and much-vaunted Messerschmitt 110, a twin-engined, two-seater escort fighter for which the Luftwaffe had great hopes. Anticipation of meeting this as yet *rara avis* was sharpened by the fact that the C-in-C had offered dinner in Paris to the first flyer to nail one of the species.

On the afternoon of the 29th Flt Lt 'Johnny' Walker led a section patrolling Metz 'Centre Front' at 20,000 feet. Number two was PO Stratton, with Clowes piloting L1969 as No.3. At 2.30 p.m. the trio

Early production MkI Hawker Hurricanes were powered by a Rolls-Royce Merlin II driving a Watts two-blade, fixed-pitch wooden airscrew. No.1 Squadron deployed these manoeuvrable 300mph monoplanes from early 1939. (Squadron Archives)

An Albion three-point petrol bowser refuels Hurricane N2358 JX-Z at Vassincourt, France, late in 1939. (Squadron Archives).

On 23 November 1939, Clowes' Hurricane was hit by an impatient French Curtiss Hawk 75A while he was attacking a Heinkel III over Saarbrücken. The impact sheared off most of his rudder, which is illustrated in this depiction of the incident. (Grub Street Publications)

sighted 'bogies' east of Metz. They resolved themselves into the shapes of twin-finned, two-motor machines, speedily identified as the new 110s. There were nine of them from V(Z)LG1, patrolling in line-astern sections of three. The interception took place over Bouzanville, and each British flier went in to fight what amounted to a private battle.

The Hurricanes went into line-astern; Clowes, at the rear, suddenly spotted two further 110s diving on the section from the right rear. He called an urgent warning on the R/T and swung right to attack, pulling round so tightly that he blacked out. He recovered at 18,000 feet in a steep dive, and on levelling out saw two 110s (presumably the pair he had originally sighted) on his tail. Arthur turned and pulled inside the *Zerstörers,* thumbing three short bursts at the leader, who pulled up, stalled onto his back and then spiralled into a vertical dive. The second Messerschmitt was still behind, but Clowes out-turned and speedily shook off his opponent. Below him was another 110 in a dive. 'Pulling the plug', he hurtled down in pursuit, the Merlin screaming in protest, but the German aircraft left him standing. Easing out of the dive, he picked out another Me 110 far on his left and 6,000 feet below. A Hurricane was in pursuit, with a second Messerschmitt on his tail. Opening the throttle again, Darky lined up the second Me from abeam, giving it a long burst from 400 and closing to below a hundred yards. The 110 broke away, diving to the left. By this time Clowes was going too fast to follow, and he plunged into cloud at 5,000 feet. The Hurricanes met up again over Metz before returning to base.

In his combat report, Clowes noted that the rear gunners of the enemy two-seaters could not apparently manipulate their MG15s in tight turns; when he was well within range of one of his opponents, he experienced no return fire. Though the 110 seemed to be much faster in a dive, it was nowhere near as manoeuvrable as a Hurricane. The wreckage of a 110 was later found, the pilot having baled out. On the same evening, according to custom, Arthur joined the other victorious pilots in ceremoniously drinking from a bottle reserved for such occasions, giving the toast 'To past members of No.1 Squadron'. They then filled in and signed the Victory Card. A party followed, ending in the Sergeants' Mess, which was a cosy room fitted up like an English country pub with a bar and beer-barrel seats.

There remained the question of the C-in-C's dinner. Walker insisted that all three pilots deserved the award, and the Bull sent a telegram to Air Marshal A.S. 'Ugly' Barratt to that effect, pointing out that the 110 was 'brought down by teamwork'. Barratt was up to the occasion. He sent his personal aircraft, a Percival Q6, to collect the trio on the 31st. They dined with the C-in-C at Maxim's on the Rue Royale, with the squadron diary recording that 'a corking good time was had by all'. So, wrote Noel Monks in his *Squadrons Up,* an 'air marshal, a flight lieutenant, a flying officer and a sergeant pilot sat down to dinner together. What price democracy?'

A relieved Sergeant Clowes shows off his damaged fighter L1842 JX-T, which he force-landed with great skill after the Curtiss Hawk had carved off most of his tail unit during his attack on the Heinkel III. (T. Humberstone)

By this time Arthur had met his future wife, Phyllis Graves, a Welsh girl, whom he married in the spring of 1940, but on 10 May, the Wehrmacht launched their *Blitzkrieg* on the West, and No.1 were soon heavily engaged with the Luftwaffe. Darky missed the early battles as he was still on leave. By late April the majority of the squadron's Hurricanes had been equipped with the latest three-blade, constant-speed propellers, which were a remarkable improvement on the old wooden-bladers with which they had started hostilities. They could now climb up to 30,000 feet and engage enemy fighters on more equal terms. Though pilots on leave were not supposedly subject to recall, Darky and others were hastily sent for when the campaign began. They arrived back on the afternoon of 13 May after quite a few delays, including the stoppage of their train 15 miles on the wrong side of Rheims, after undergoing several bouts of bombing. Heavily engaged in the early fighting, the rest of the unit had given a good account of themselves after their removal to Berry-au-Bac, 30 miles to the north-west of Rheims, on the afternoon of 10 May.

Clowes was back in action on 14 May with 'A' Flight, though unfortunately his combat reports for the rest of the French campaign have not survived, along with most of No.1's records for this period. His engagements have been pieced together from several sources. 'A' Flight was assigned to escort a formation of Battles, bombing advanced units of the Wehrmacht, but ran headlong into a mass of Junkers 87 dive bombers, protected by Me 109s. The Hurricanes hit the Messerschmitts first, Darky shooting down one machine from 4/JG53 and then added a *Stuka* of 2/StG77, which crashed in the

Chesne area, to his tally. The victorious detachment then broke off the engagement to see the Battles home. It was the only time No.1 met the vulnerable dive-bombers whilst in France.

The following day 'A' Flight were scrambled to meet an incoming raid on Vouziers. The six Hurricanes met some 150 Luftwaffe aircraft, comprising forty Dornier 17s at 10,000 feet, protected by massed squadrons of Messerschmitt 110s stacked up to 18,000 feet, all heading straight for the pitifully few attackers. 'Johnny' Walker led the flight around the right flank of the huge swarm of enemy aeroplanes, climbing hard to gain height above the topmost level of the escorts. Sighting the Hurricanes as they dived to attack, the German top cover formed a defensive circle, which was broken up by 'A' Flight in a series of individual attacks. Darky shot down one Me 110 in the mêlée, from 111/ZG26, whilst several others plunged away to destruction before the surviving Hurricanes managed to break off the combat. Two of their number were destroyed, with FO Paul Richey baling out with his glycol tank on fire and Walker force-landing with a dead engine.

The unit moved again on the following day, 15 May, to Vraux, halfway between Rheims and Paris. By the 18th they were 30 miles to the south-west of Anglure, still flying and fighting. Anglure was simply a collection of fields rolled flat where necessary and surrounded by standing crops, and 501 Squadron were also stationed there. After further heroic actions on the 19th, Halahan realised that the majority of his pilots

Boys will be boys! Sqn Ldr 'Bull' Halahan, the unit's charismatic commander, plays with an MG15 machine gun liberated from a shot-down Dornier 17. Paul Richey points out the salient features of the weapon, whilst Darky Clowes looks on with interest. (Squadron Archives)

Above: *Arthur Clowes
battled with Messerschmitt
110 escort fighters on a
number of occasions. He
first met them near Metz on
29 March 1940, when they
were still an unknown
quantity.*

Left: *Clowes' fourth aerial
victim was a Junkers 87B
of 2/StG77, which he shot
down over Chesne on
14 May, 1940. It was the
only time he engaged the
vulnerable dive-bombers in the
air. It was similar to the one
in the illustration.*

Opposite above: *Arthur
intercepted Dornier 17Z
raiders like the one shown
here of 3/ZG2 over
Chelmsford on 31 August
1940, when he claimed two
probable victims.*

Above: *Darky Clowes enters the cockpit of his stalwart Hurricane P3395 JX-B, snug in its blast pen at RAF Collyweston in the autumn of 1940. Note the paintwork under the cockpit, scuffed to bare metal, the small square anti-gas panel on the wing. No.1's Hurricanes had bands painted on their spinners, perhaps colour-coded to identify the various sections.* (Squadron Archives)

were at the end of their tether and asked permission to withdraw them. Surprisingly his request was granted, and most of the experienced members of the squadron were speedily repatriated. An equally surprising fact was that Clowes was left to soldier on, accompanied only by newly-promoted Flt Lt 'Hilly' Brown. It was obviously felt that Arthur's combat expertise was indispensable in helping to train the new flyers drafted in to replace the war-fatigued veterans who had gone home. No.1 now had a new CO, Sqn Ldr Pemberton. Apart from Brown and Clowes, and a nucleus who had already been blooded, the unit now consisted of tenderfeet, fresh from the training schools.

On 23 May Darky and FO Thom were supervising the refuelling of their mounts when a Heinkel III droned overhead. The pair leapt into their Hurricanes and gave chase, catching up with the raider near Rouen. They were joined by Flt Lt Warcup en route and took turns in individual attacks until the Heinkel, trailing smoke and with wheels down indicating its hydraulics had gone, lost height through low cloud and subsequently crashed. Whilst hammering the bomber from astern, Clowes affirmed that the rear gunner 'fired what appeared to be a stream of mesh netting intended to enmesh the airscrew'.

No.1 endured further moves westwards across France during the first part of June as their ally's resistance gradually crumbled. On the 13th they were stationed near Caen, patrolling the Seine and covering the evacuation of troops from Le Havre. The next day Clowes led the last section out of the airfield on the way south to Angers. Five Messerschmitt 109s appeared and in the ensuing combat he shot down one from 3/JG54, which crashed near Evreux. As the section reformed, he saw three further 109s above. He climbed to attack, damaging one which broke away in alarm. The other two Messerschmitts took immediate cover in convenient clouds.

The squadron's French sojourn was now almost at its end. On the morning of 18 June, the twelve surviving Hurricanes roared off from their last base at Nantes, refuelling on the way at Jersey and reaching their old home, Tangmere, in the early afternoon. They had been the first unit to fly to France and were one of the very last to leave. On 11 July, Darky was awarded a Mention in Despatches, and in the high summer of 1940, in the middle of the Battle of Britain, he and twelve other squadron veterans were the recipients of a unique block award of decorations for gallantry. Clowes received the Distinguished Flying Medal, given for 'courage and determination in many combats against the enemy'. The citation credited him with the destruction of at least six German aircraft, and remarked that the Derbyshire aviator 'has displayed great skill and powers of leadership'.

Clowes' unit moved to Northolt in west London after their return from the Continent, and with new aircraft and reunited with their ground crew, they began the task of bringing No.1 back to fighting trim. Sqn Ldr Pemberton instituted a period of intensive air training, and the rejuvenated squadron became operational again at the beginning of July. Though they were involved in several combats in July and August as the pace of German aerial attacks on England intensified, Arthur did not fire his guns in action until 16 August. At 4.30 p.m. on this day, Pemberton led the six Hurricanes of 'A' Flight from their Northolt base to their old peacetime HQ, Tangmere, with 'B' Flight following them five minutes later. Darky was leading Yellow Section in P3169 JX-T, and, together with Brown, was the unit's longest-serving combat veteran; a battle-honed expert in tactics and survival. Near Guildford the Hurricanes met some 100 Heinkel IIIs in stepped-up waves, with Junkers 88s behind, and Messerschmitt 110s providing a close escort. Yellow Section followed Red into the attack at 5.15 p.m. at around 18,000 feet. Clowes saw one of the twin-engined enemy bombers fall away from the leading group as Red Section broke away, one of the crewmen baling out. Lining his reflector gunsight on the abundant targets ahead, he raked the flank of the bomber stream. His tracer hosed into the glazed nose of his target and he saw lights sparkling across the perspex as his De Wilde incendiary rounds struck home. It was the first time he had used incendiary ammunition, and the effect was fairly spectacular. As he half-rolled on the break, he saw his victim slide out of line and stand on its nose, disappearing in a vertical death-dive.

Turning rapidly, Arthur bored in again for a repeat attack on the leading formation of Heinkels, though this time his fire showed no apparent result. He broke away through a layer of cloud and picked

Right: *Darky, wearing trademark white overalls and scarf, stands under the nose of P3395, adorned with the self-painted fearsome striped wasp emblem. Each black stripe represented a confirmed kill.* (Squadron Archives)

Below: *No.1 Squadron pilots line up at Wittering in November 1940. From left to right, back row: Clowes, Zavoral, Prihoda, Elkington. Centre row: Demozay, Kuttelwascher, Novak, Stefan. Front row: Hancock, Brown (CO), Chetam, Plasil. Between them, Clowes, Demozay, Kuttelwascher and Brown accounted for some 70 Axis warplanes.* (Squadron Archives)

up a single bomber heading south below him. He went into a stern chase, catching up with his adversary, which he identified as a Junkers 88, but which in fact was a Heinkel IIIP of 4/KG55. His eight Brownings sprayed out an opening burst as he closed from abeam, and the startled enemy pilot nosed his heavy machine over into a dive. Four 602 Squadron Spitfires suddenly appeared on the scene, and evidently regarding discretion as the better part of valour, the Heinkel chose a large field at Upper Frithwold Farm. It was near Petworth, a few miles north of Bognor Regis, and with its hydraulics probably shot up, the bomber, coded G1+LM, brought off a successful crash-landing. As Darky circled overhead, four crew members struggled from their wrecked aeroplane. He was not to know as he turned away for base that the downed bomber suddenly and violently exploded, killing the unfortunate German airmen clustered around it. A complete starboard wing, bearing the black cross and letter L was found a mile away in 1973 and is now in Tangmere Museum. Back at base the Derbyshire flier was credited with a Heinkel III and a Junkers 88 destroyed.

There were two days of frantic activity at the end of the month. By this time Clowes had taken over Hurricane P3395 JX-B, an aircraft he flew for the rest of the Battle. It has since been depicted in a number of aviation publications, plus *The Illustrated London News* of 16 November 1940, as well as appearing as a 1/72 scale Airfix plastic model. This distinctive aeroplane, bearing a narrow yellow band painted round the spinner of its Rotol airscrew, carried its own logo – a fearsome black-striped yellow wasp, which appeared on both sides of the engine cowling below the exhaust stubs. Arthur had some skill as an artist, and his family in Canada have several of his watercolours. Each stripe on the wasp represented a confirmed kill. Over fifty years later, a Hurricane Mk IV could be seen masquerading as Clowes' P3395 and was exhibited on Horse Guards Parade in London during the Battle's fiftieth anniversary celebrations in September 1990.

A charcoal portrait of Flight Lieutenant Clowes DFM, drawn by Cuthbert Orde on 22 February 1941. (T. Humberstone)

Clowes' first action in P3395 took place on 30 August when No.1 Squadron were scrambled to intercept a raid over Essex. An untidy shoal of some thirty Heinkel IIIs hove into view, accompanied by an equally dispersed group of Messerschmitt 110s, the whole ragged assemblage giving the impression of having already been in action. Darky, Yellow 1, reported the hostiles over Epping to Control just before 5 p.m. There was a leading gaggle of 111s fairly close together at 11,000 feet, followed by twenty or thirty stragglers at up to 15,000, with fifty to sixty 110s above them. His immediate target was an escort fighter, which he curved in behind, thumbing off a short burst at 250 yards that struck home in the raider's starboard motor. The Me 110 broke away, trailing coolant vapour. Ahead were three 111s at 12,000 feet. He opened up on one which began emitting black smoke and flame. He switched his attack to a second victim at 250 yards, seeing the glazed nose of his target literally explode as the perspex disintegrated under the cone of fire from his eight .303 Brownings. Further game abounded; at 10,000 feet he fell in behind a Dornier 17, which he attacked without result. The clatter of empty breech blocks told him he was out of ammunition and he broke away for home, claiming two Heinkel IIIs and a Messerschmitt 110 damaged.

'Home is the Hunter.' Squadron Leader Arthur Clowes' flag-draped coffin is laid to rest with full military honours in the churchyard of St Mary Magdalene at Brampton, Huntingdon, on 10 December 1949. (T. Humberstone)

There was little time for rest and respite. At 7.40 a.m. the next day, No.1 were scrambled to patrol over Chelmsford. Once again leading Yellow Section in JX-B, flying north-east at 8.10 a.m., Clowes picked out a swarm of enemy bombers, Dornier 17s and Junkers 88s, shepherded by dozens of Messerschmitt 110s in line-astern. Initially he could not engage the bombers for fear of the escorts hovering above. Finally he led his section in a climbing frontal attack on fifteen Dorniers coming on in five vics of three aircraft each. He managed a brief two-second burst, then half-rolled and climbed to repeat the dose. Only thirteen Dorniers were still in formation. Another was spinning down dragging smoke, whilst a second was falling out of the group in a steep, left-hand turn. These aircraft were probably Do 17Zs of 3/KG2 on the way to bomb RAF Debden. The Staff Flight of this unit were attacked head-on by a lone Hurricane, and U5+BD dived away, exposing the Gruppe Commander's machine U5+AD to a burst of fire which wounded the CO, Major Fuchs. Both Dorniers regained the safety of France.

A section of 110s appeared above and behind, and Arthur looped up into them from below. Framing one in his reflector, he released a short burst at long range and saw its starboard engine spraying out white smoke. The 110 stayed in formation, but then Clowes saw its propeller windmill as the motor died. Closing on his quarry, he hammered out another burst and the *Zerstörer* dived away to ground level, with P3395 hanging on close behind. As the twin-engined escort levelled out, its speed fell dramatically, Clowes hosing his target liberally with short bursts until his ammunition was exhausted. He felt he had killed the rear gunner and, as he departed the scene, his impression was that the pilot 'appeared to be looking for a place to land near Martlesham'. His opponent was probably a 110 of 14(Z)LG1, two of whose aircraft were lost over the Thames Estuary that morning. L1+LK had its

The simple marble cross marks the last resting place of Derbyshire's foremost fighter ace of the Second World War. (Author)

starboard engine knocked out and rear gunner Unteroffizier Growe killed; the pilot, Leutnant Eichhorn, struggled back across the estuary before the other motor failed and he ditched off Margate. A second aircraft, L1+AK, was shot up by a Hurricane, which set its port DB601 motor afire and stopped its partner. The fighter crashed into the sea between Foulness and the Isle of Sheppey, though both crewmen, Feldwebel Fritz and Obergefreiter Dopfer, survived. Though there seems little doubt that one of these escorts was Arthur's victim, he was only able to claim a probable 110 during this fast-moving and lively early-morning foray.

By early September, No.1 Squadron was still a fairly intact, though very tired, unit, with each pilot having flown an average of two operational sorties per day over many weeks. Darky flew as many as anyone, and on more than one occasion his skills had prevented casualties. On 6 September he led the squadron for the first time as 'Hilly' Brown's engine failed to start. The Hurricanes scrambled at 1 p.m. to intercept an incoming raid on London from the direction of Dungeness. Whilst climbing, a gaggle of Me 109s came down like a flock of vicious birds, but Arthur 'fought a brilliant defensive action', shepherding his charges safely through the enemy attack. On the following day, No.1 were led off on a late-afternoon sortie over north-east London. Scrambling at 4.25 p.m. the eleven Hurricanes met up with the enemy at 5 p.m. Clowes, Yellow Leader, noticed a large concentration of bombers flanked by a whole hive of some one hundred 109s and 110s. The entire mass were heading north-west until they saw the Hurricanes, whereupon they wheeled south-west. Clowes carried out ineffective attacks on several enemy fighters as the formation swung round. One attack led him as far east as Manston. Finally, he slid behind an unsuspecting Me 110 at 13,000 feet, targeting his slim, twin-finned quarry in his gunsight. He fired two concentrated bursts of two seconds each, seeing his tracer hit home. The stricken escort nosed over in a terminal dive and crashed into the sea off the Kent coast in a great cloud of spray. In his various brushes with the foe, Arthur's keen eye noted that some of the two-seaters had white-painted noses, the distinguishing mark of ZG26. His victim may have been Me 110C-4 A2+ML (3570) of 6/ZG2, which ditched off Birchington at 5.20 p.m. The pilot, Oberleutnant Brede, survived, though his gunner, Unteroffizier Galla, was killed.

By this time the squadron were showing marked signs of fatigue, resulting from their long period in 11 Group's front line. Fortunately they were scheduled for a rest, and on 9 September they were posted to Wittering in a quiet sector of 12 Group. They were dispersed to the satellite airstrip of Collyweston, and the fliers were able to relax and anticipate leave for the first time in weeks. Arthur Clowes' dedication, commitment and leadership were recognised by the well-deserved, if belated, granting of a commission on 13 September. In fact, he progressed so rapidly through the lower officer ranks that he caught up with pilots who had been officers since before the war, when he was a lowly sergeant. In six weeks he advanced from sergeant to flight lieutenant in charge of 'A' Flight. It is thought that he was promoted so rapidly that he never actually held the rank of flying officer!

Darky's final combat with the unit he had served with such distinction took place on 24 October. He was flying his faithful P3395 as Red 2 to 'Hilly' Brown on a patrol in search of a lone bandit, with PO Kershaw occupying the Red 3 slot. The enemy raider, that *rara avis* a Dornier 215B, was intercepted at 12.04 p.m., east of Banbury, at 3,000 feet above cloud and heading west. The Dornier dived away as the pilot saw Nemesis approaching, and Darky was the first to attack. He came in from above and behind to deliver a burst as he closed from 300 to 100 yards, and down to zero deflection. He noticed return fire as he broke away to allow Red 1 to follow him in. Brown fired a series of bursts as the 215 plunged away in search of cloud cover. All the RAF pilots were critical of the German's tactics; there was eight-tenths cloud cover, stretching from 3,000 to 6,000 feet, and he was very late in going for it. The enemy raider – from 3/Aufklarungs Gruppe ObdL, Wn. 0060, and coded L2+KS – was on a photographic reconnaissance sortie to Coventry and Birmingham. It crashed at Eaton Socon, near St Neots, at 12.35 p.m. All four crew baled out, but three of them left it too late and were killed. A fourth was wounded, but survived the low drop. Interestingly, an MG15 machine gun, which was jettisoned from the enemy aeroplane, was picked up near Towcester. This action was the last occasion on which Arthur engaged the enemy in the air.

Flight Lieutenant Clowes served with No.1 until April 1941. On New Year's Eve 1940 he was briefed to lead four aircraft in a 'mosquito raid' (later to be called a 'rhubarb'), attacking enemy ground defences between Calais and Dunkirk. Flying Hurricane V6935 and accompanied by POs Lewis and Kershaw, the trio took off at 10.50 a.m. from Hawkinge. The fourth pilot had an argument with a Spitfire on the perimeter track and had to abort. Clowes' Merlin began running roughly and the section turned for home. The engine then cleared itself and they swept back at 1,500 feet under ten-tenths cloud, separating in the murk to attack individual objectives. Darky strafed some military transport

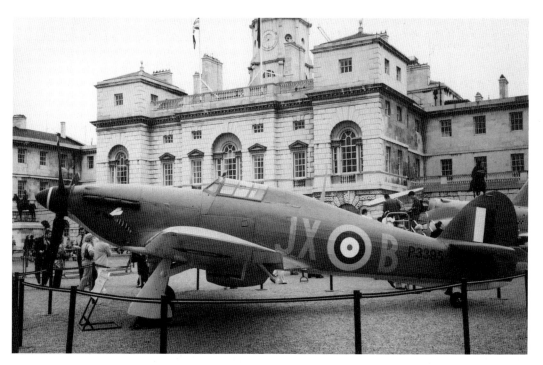

A Hurricane Mk IV from the Birmingham Museum of Science and Industry masquerades as Darky Clowes' P3395 on Horse Guards Parade on 15 September 1990, the fiftieth Anniversary of the Battle of Britain. (Author)

without any observable results, before returning at 12.30 p.m. The other pilots also attacked targets of opportunity in the improving conditions. Though only a minor operation, these low-level flights became commonplace over the next few months, and despite doubts as to their cost-effectiveness, No.1 did feel they had begun to hit back, only six months after they had been driven from France.

Arthur's time with his beloved unit was almost up. The only other excitement was a crash-landing in Hurricane V7025 after an engine failure, following a patrol over Maidstone. His long association with the squadron was severed on 23 April, St George's Day, when he was posted to No.56 OTU at Sutton Bridge. Six days later his outstanding service was rewarded with a well-merited Distinguished Flying Cross to add to the ribbon of the DFM he wore under his wings. The citation read:

> This officer has displayed great skill in his engagements against the enemy, and has destroyed at least eleven of their aircraft. His coolness and judgement on all occasions have been an inspiration to his fellow pilots.

The rest of Darky Clowes' war was something of an anticlimax. He served with Nos 56 and 53 OTUs before his promotion to Squadron Leader in December 1941, to command No.79 Squadron. When this unit embarked for India, he was posted to several staff appointments in the Middle East. In August 1942 he took over 601 Squadron in the Western Desert, leading them for three months before joining Middle East HQ as Senior Controller in charge of Sector Operations. He only led one further squadron, No.94, when it was serving in an Eastern Mediterranean backwater in 1943, and he returned late in 1943 for further HQ and administrative duties. He lost his left eye when abroad, in an accident apparently suffered during a bout of high spirits in the mess. This accident effectively put an end to his flying career and for the rest of his life he was grounded in a series of administrative posts. Billy Drake, a fellow pilot in No.1 Squadron and later a colleague serving with him in the Western Desert, recalled that Arthur suffered from narcolepsy 'and would on occasion suddenly fall asleep into his soup when at the meal table, or on other similarly inappropriate and embarrassing occasions'.

Philip Sanders met Squadron Leader Clowes after the war when the pair were seconded to the Air Ministry. He remembered Arthur as 'a good type, and a character'. He remained a squadron leader until his untimely death, and his last posting was to HQ, Technical Training Command at Brampton Grange near Huntingdon. Arthur attended the dedication of the Battle of Britain Commemorative Window at the Rolls-Royce factory in Derby on 11 January 1949. Tragically, this brave, skilled and tenacious warrior contracted cancer of the liver and died in the RAF Hospital, Ely, less than eleven months later, on 7 December, at the young age of thirty-seven. He was buried with full military honours in the quiet churchyard of St Mary Magdalene, Brampton, three days later. On the marble cross forming his memorial is the simple inscription:

Squadron Leader A.V. Clowes DFC DFM
Royal Air Force
1912-1949

A number of misconceptions have arisen over the years concerning Arthur Victor Clowes, which relate to his origins, rank and decorations. This account sets the record straight, and pays due tribute to a son of Derbyshire who rose from humble beginnings to become the county's leading fighter pilot of the Second World War; a man respected and admired by his peers, who gained promotion on merit, and who occupies a special place in the annals of No.1 Squadron. Like his beloved unit, Arthur Victor Clowes was truly a man 'first in all things'.

two

Flight Lieutenant
Norman Taylor
DFC DFM

Combat Record

Date	Sqn	Locality	Aircraft Flown	Enemy Type	Claim
15.08.40	601	S. of Spithead	Hurricane I P3393	Junkers 88	Destroyed (shared)
16.08.40	601	Selsey Bill	Hurricane I P3393	Junkers 88A	Probable
18.08.40	601	Thorney Island	Hurricane I P3393	Junkers 87B	Destroyed
30.08.40	601	Hunsdon	Hurricane I P3735	Heinkel IIIH	Destroyed (shared)
31.08.40	601	Gravesend	Hurricane I P3735	Messerschmitt 109E	Destroyed
04.09.40	601	Worthing	Hurricane I V6632	Dornier 17Z	Damaged
06.09.40	601	Tunbridge Wells	Hurricane I V6632	Dornier 17Z	Destroyed
07.10.40	601	Portland	Hurricane I V6632	Messerschmitt 110	Damaged
25.05.41	601	Calais Calais	Hurricane IIB Z3030	Messerschmitt 110 Messerschmitt 109E	Destroyed Destroyed
13.06.41	601	Dover Dover	Hurricane IIB Z2745	Messerschmitt 109F Messerschmitt 109F	Destroyed Destroyed
16.06.41	601	Off Dover	Hurricane IIB Z2745	Messerschmitt 109E	Damaged
01.11.42	MSFU	250m W. of Spanish coast	Sea Hurricane IA V7070	Focke-Wulf 200C	Destroyed

Flight Lieutenant Norman Taylor DFC DFM

NORMAN TAYLOR shares the distinction of being one of Derbyshire's foremost fighter pilots of the Second World War along with Darky Clowes. His claims for enemy warplanes destroyed or 'probable' run into double figures, and he is the only county airman known to have shot down a four-engined German aircraft. His combat career falls neatly into two phases – eleven months' honourable service with 601 Squadron during 1940-41, followed by an equally celebrated period as a flyer with the Merchant Ship Fighter Unit (MSFU), operating Camship Hurricanes from merchantmen in the mid-Atlantic against long-range enemy reconnaissance bombers.

Norman was born in October 1920, the only son of George and Minnie Taylor of Chellaston, though he did have four sisters with whom to contend. His early schooling was at the then small village of Melbourne Council School, at St James Road School, Derby, and at Ashby Grammar School, Leicestershire, before a family move to Kenilworth took him to Coventry's Bablake Technical School. Norman's interests were practical, and at sixteen-and-a-half he became an apprentice at the Standard Motor Company with the eventual ambition of test flying. At the age of nineteen he joined the RAFVR, being granted leave from his apprenticeship to undertake a two-month course in *ab initio* flying training. This was at the No.11 Elementary & Reserve Flying Training School at Prestwick, Ayr. Norman's introduction to flying under instruction was in Tiger Moth G-AFFA on 30 March 1939, first soloing (after 10 hours' dual) in L6949 on 24 April. He completed 50 hours in the air and 3 hours in the Link trainer on the comprehensive Prestwick course, and on 26 May gained an 'Average' pass.

Norman then suffered the rigours meted out at No.3 Initial Training Wing at RAF St Leonard's-on-Sea, and returned to resume his apprenticeship whilst awaiting a posting to a Service Flying Training School. Fortunately he was able to fly more advanced Hart and Hind biplane trainers at weekends with No.9 E&RFTS at Ansty, completing their course in late August. On 7 March 1940 Taylor reported to No.10 SFTS at Ternhill, Shropshire, for instruction on Harvard low-wing monoplanes. The Harvard incorporated refinements such as a retractable undercarriage and a variable-pitch propeller. Soloing in a Harvard by the 15th, with 65 flying hours in his logbook, Norman found there was still much to assimilate: map-reading, formation and instrument flying, navigation, night exercises, air-to-ground firing and dive-bombing practice, war-load climbs, and a variety of flying techniques. On 7 June, piloting Harvard N7016 on an air-to-ground firing exercise, the throttle of his Pratt & Whitney Wasp radial jammed at 400 feet. He brought off a successful crash-landing, just managing to scramble clear before the aeroplane caught fire and rapidly burned out.

Practice operations remained the main fare throughout the early summer of 1940. Taylor completed the advanced course on 27 June, having amassed a total flying time of 167 hours. His assessment was rated for the first time as 'Above Average' and he moved on to No.6 Operational Training Unit a happy man. Here, at Sutton Bridge, a few miles west of Kings Lynn, he honed his skills and expertise on Hurricane fighters, gaining a valuable 34 hours on the type. This was a vital bonus as after a short leave he was posted to 601 Squadron, AAF on 7 August, which was just in time to participate in the main stages of the Battle of Britain.

601 Squadron, based at Tangmere on the Sussex coast in 11 Group, was an auxiliary unit, formed before the war and staffed mainly with well-to-do part-time fliers, whose exemplification of the AAF spirit included an aversion to pomposity and an irreverent disregard for rules and regulations. The pre-war AAF was rather like a gentleman's club, where family atmosphere and status were paramount. However, though the keynote of the amateurs was individualist, they were bound together by a self-imposed disciplinary code which made them extremely effective once war began. 601 became popularly known as the 'Millionaire's Squadron', although they preferred their own designation, the 'Legion.' Most of the pre-war pilots owned their own aeroplanes, though by the time Taylor entered their ranks as a sergeant pilot, a general leavening, caused by combat losses over

TEN LITTLE FICHTER BOYS

Ten Little Fighter boys taking off in Line
One was in coarse pitch, then there were nine
Nine little fighter boys climbing through the gate
One's petrol wasn't on, then there were eight
Eight little fighter boys scrambling up to heaven
One weaver didn't and then there were seven
Seven little fighter boys up to all the tricks
One had a hangover then there were six
Six little fighter boys milling over Hythe
One's pressure wasn't up and then there were five
Five little fighter boys over France's shore
One flew reciprocal and then there were four
Four little fighter boys joining in the spree
One's sight wasn't on and then there were three
Three little fighter boys high up in the blue
One's rubber pipe was loose then there were two
Two little fighter boys homing out of sun
Flew straight and level and then there was one
One little fighter boy happy to be home
Beat up dispersal and then there were none
Ten little Spitfires nothing have achieved
A.O.C at Group is very very peeved
"Fifty thousand Smackers thrown down the drains
'Cause Ten Silly baskets didn't use their brains

'Ten Little Fighter Boys' (pasted into the logbook of Norman Taylor).

32

France and an injection of NCO pilots, had blunted its more class-bound edge. Their commanding officer, Sqn Ldr Max Aitken, the son of Lord Beaverbrook, was preparing the Legion to meet the main thrust of the Luftwaffe, by then massed on French airfields immediately across the Channel from Tangmere.

Norman's first mission was not long in coming: on 15 August the squadron were in action intercepting an incoming raid approaching Portsmouth. 601 took off as part of an eight-squadron concentration of Spitfires and Hurricanes, who waylaid some 300 enemy aircraft over the Channel during the afternoon. Flying P3393 in the Blue 2 slot at 5.40 p.m., 17,000 feet over Bishop's Waltham, Norman picked out twelve Junkers 88 bombers in close vic formation heading towards Portsmouth. Blue Section flew alongside the raiders until they had overhauled the leader, whereupon the green-and-brown camouflaged warplanes swung in to attack from abeam. Taylor joined in a close-range spraying of the outside bombers, only breaking away when within handshaking distance of his target. One victim fell away with part of its starboard wing blown off, Norman dosing it with a three-second burst from his close-grouped Brownings as he followed it down. He saw its port motor splutter to a stop and its propeller windmilling. He could not confirm its inevitable demise as he was busy coping with an Me 109 which he found on his tail, and which took some shaking off.

Taylor then located four more Ju 88s heading towards Winchester, but he was unable to attack as four Hurricanes were busy using the German machines for target practice. He noticed two parachutes descending, but could not make out whether the aircrew were British or hostile. He subsequently recorded that 'the whole formation had been well broken up and what were left did not have much time to concentrate on bombing because they were turning in all directions.' The Derbyshire pilot returned to base, landing at Tangmere at 6.25 p.m., having loosed off some 1,200 rounds of ammunition.

On the following day, at around 2.00 p.m., a large force of Junkers 87B dive-bombers winged in over the English coast 2 miles east of Selsey Bill heading for Tangmere. 601 intercepted the raid and though some damage was done to airfield buildings, the *Stukas* paid heavily for their success. During the combat, Norman, flying P3393, met a Junkers 88 near Selsey, claiming a 'probable' over the coast. After fruitless patrols on a quiet 17 August, the unit faced a mass attack the following day, led by their new CO, Sqn Ldr Sir Archibald Hope.

The Legion met some sixty *Stukas* of StG77, protected by fifteen Messerschmitt 109s over Thorney Island at around 2.00 p.m. on the afternoon of 18 August. Accompanied by 43, Squadron 601 weaved in among the slow, crank-winged two-seaters with their fixed, spatted undercarriages, and did considerable execution. Norman, flying as Blue 2, came across some fifty or so dive bombers over Selsey Bill at 12,000 feet, screened by Me 109s above and behind. His section dived on a group of dark green *Stukas,* squeezing off short bursts and causing the enemy formation to break up. As they scattered, he dived again, on three Ju 87s hanging together in a close vic. He framed one of the warplanes in the glowing ring of his reflector and thumbed off a long burst, closing to within 100 yards of the German machine. His quarry went into a steep dive, followed by a second bomber, and Taylor saw it tumble to earth. He could not substantiate the end of the second *Stuka*, though he reported that 'if it did not crash it certainly must have been damaged'. He was then distracted by 'a 109 on my tail who put a few bullets in my fuselage', including one which penetrated his starboard mainplane. Two other NCOs from the unit were shot down and killed by 109s of JG27, and a third crash-landed at base. The Derbyshire flyer was presumably a near victim of this outfit. He landed back at base at 2.35 p.m., having expended some 2,000 rounds. He subsequently reported that the hovering Messerschmitts appeared to wait until the Hurricanes dived onto the Ju 87s, whereupon they pursued them down. Norman flew three further sorties that day, ending in a chase after a Heinkel 59 floatplane, over the Channel, which Green 1 attacked without success.

On 19 August Taylor chased a lone Junkers 88 without getting near the raider, flogging P3393 at speeds of up to 350mph, according to his log. On the 20th the tired unit were moved from the front line, exchanging duties with 17 Squadron and relocating to Debden, south-east of Cambridge, though his own flight spent some time at Martlesham near Ipswich. Here, in a supposed rest area, they commenced convoy patrols with occasional visits back to Debden. On the 23rd, in P3735, Norman chased a Dornier 17 into cloud, but until the very end of the month, whilst Goering pounded 11 Group's airfields, things remained fairly peaceful for the Legion.

On 30 August at 4.30 p.m., the squadron were vectored onto a Heinkel III-H formation from KG53, heading for the Handley-Page aircraft factory at Radlett to the north of London, with Taylor piloting P3735 in the Blue 3 position. The raiders were badly savaged, losing no less than six of their number to fighter attacks. Four Hurricanes of 'B' Flight, including Taylor's, repeatedly assaulted a machine from the 7th Staffel, coded A1+CR, knocking out the starboard motor. As the stricken bomber lost height for a crash-landing, the overworked port engine began disgorging flames and smoke. The Heinkel caught fire and smashed down hard in a field near Hunsdon, to the north-west of Harlow. Two of the crew were killed and two wounded, with only one escaping without injury. Norman was allotted a quarter-share of the victory.

Next day he was in action again, at 1.15 p.m. over the Thames Estuary, catching an incoming raid whilst flying as Blue 3 in P3735 on a patrol over Colchester. At 10,000 feet east of Tilbury, the squadron picked out a whole swarm of bandits flying west at Angels 15, comprising two formations of Dornier 17s in close vics, with dozens of Me 109s above them in sections of three. As the 601 pilots revved their Merlins hard to gain height, Taylor saw accurate ack-ack bursts explode among the raiders, scattering the bombers and leaving stragglers astern of the main mass. Blue Section went into line-astern to close the Dorniers, with Norman some way behind his numbers one and two. Suddenly a Messerschmitt 109 came down from above and hung in front of his nose, as though intent on attacking his comrades ahead. Norman later felt the 109 was a decoy, deliberately flying in front of him to set him up for his wingman, but it seems more likely that the German pilot was a victim of the notoriously poor view from his aeroplane's cockpit, and simply failed to see the lagging Hurricane as he went for the leading pair in Blue Section. Whatever the circumstances, the 1/JG77 fighter, Wn. 6092, flown by Feldwebel Kramer, took a lethal burst from the Derbyshireman's eight Brownings, but Taylor immediately felt hits smashing into his own machine from astern, as Kramer's number two lined up the Hurricane in his sights. In quick succession, the gravity tank in front of him was holed, petrol sprayed into his unprotected face temporarily blinding him, and his fighter went into a spin. He was extremely lucky that no spark ignited the fuel and set his cockpit ablaze. Norman applied opposite rudder to try and right the gyration, but more fire struck his aircraft, which nosed over into a dive, persuading him it was time to leave. He released his safety straps and fell into space, 18,000 feet over Gravesend, one of three Legion pilots to hit the silk in the same combat. His Irvin parachute No. 47445 safely bore him to earth 2 miles east of Gravesend, and he duly claimed his badge from the Caterpillar Club for the successful drop. On landing, he had absolutely no idea that the 109 he had attacked had force-landed not far from an army barracks at nearby Shornmead Fort until he was given confirmation, not only by soldiers helping him out of his harness, but by the Intelligence Officer from the nearby airfield. The enemy pilot was severely burned in the crash; a clock removed from the wreckage at the time was subsequently placed with the Hawkinge Aeronautical Trust. Norman wrote in his logbook: 'Went to see the pilot of the Me 109. He was badly burnt'. In fact, the luckless feldwebel had severe injuries to his face, arms and back.

In early September the combat-worn unit were sent back to Tangmere. On the 4th Taylor was patrolling Worthing in Hurricane V6632, and on returning to base came up against a shoal of Dornier 17s, shepherded by Messerschmitt 110s. Diving through the formation, he targeted one of the bombers, hitting it hard enough to claim a 'damaged' on landing. Two days later the squadron were involved in a running combat across Kent at 9.30 a.m. in which they lost four Hurricanes. Two of the pilots, the stalwarts Willie Rhodes-Moorhouse DFC and Carl Davis DFC, an American volunteer, were killed. Flying V6632 as Blue 3, Norman reported that his section were patrolling Maidstone at 20,000 feet when a Me 109 crossed in front of the leader's Hurricane. The section split up, and Taylor headed south, espying some thirty Dornier 17s at 15,000 feet in a ragged-looking gaggle, as though they had been previously attacked. Completely alone, he called up Control to report the raiders, but got no response. He then picked out a straggler from the broken-up formation, and 'pieces flew off in all directions' under his concentrated fire. As he contemplated a further attack, Norman suffered palpitations as an unnoticed fighter came up from behind and fastened on to his tail. With great relief he identified his pursuer as another Hurricane! No Dornier 17s are recorded as RAF victims that day, but several Me 110s fell in combat, and he may well have destroyed one of those. The crippling losses sustained by 601 on 6 September – two other pilots were wounded – convinced higher command that the squadron had shot its bolt and was due for complete rest and recuperation. Accordingly the depleted unit was put on the 'C' List and posted to Exeter.

In the south-west, 601 Squadron (now in 10 Group and classed as resting and under training) attracted an influx of raw flyers, fresh from the OTUs and in need of operational experience. Norman recorded his duties in September as 'training new pupils.' He became leader of Green Section, heading formation flights and patrols. The dull round now replaced the constant scrambles and the battles against odds he had been fighting ever since August. On 7 October, still piloting his faithful V6632, he damaged an Me 110, probably of ZG26, on a

A studio portrait of Pilot Officer Norman Taylor DFM, shortly after gaining his commission in summer 1941. (S. Ratledge)

patrol over Portland. In the same battle a fellow Derbyshireman, Alan Feary of 609 Squadron, fell to his death a few miles to the east, when baling out too low from his stricken Spitfire.

Contact with the Luftwaffe tailed off that month, and night flying and convoy patrols were added to the unit menu. Flying Hurricane V7236 on 17 October, Norman recorded 'Operational T/O. Patrol Plymouth 20,000ft. AA fire very good <u>at us</u>'. Bandits were rarely seen and even more rarely engaged. Norman was now a combat-hardened veteran – a stalwart of the Legion, sometimes leading his flight in the air. He did not fire his guns in anger again in 1940, and from 13 December until 7 February 1941 was off flying, enjoying a well-deserved grounding.

Taylor was happy to be back with the squadron in the New Year, flying his first sortie in his beloved V6632 on 14 February. The unit were now at Northolt under their new CO, Sqn Ldr J.A. O'Neill. On the 23rd they acted as close escort to an early Circus, accompanying Blenheims in a bombing raid on Calais. Seventy-two fighters protected the twelve bombers; no enemy aircraft were seen, though flak was both heavy and accurate. This mission set the pattern for the coming month, and Norman's log records a series of sweeps, escorts and 'rhubarbs'.

The more powerful twelve-gun Hurricane IIBs became available from early March, 601 being one of the first squadrons to re-equip with the improved warplane. Enemy aircraft remained scarce, and his only excitement was a 'rhubarb' on the 29th, flying Z2818 from Manston to Belgium. His flight crossed the coast above cloud, emerging over Ghent. Roaring over the streets of the town at low altitude, they hit the coast at Knocke, strafing a German flak ship with their multiple

At Tangmere in July 1940, 601 Squadron Hurricanes are refuelled under the watchful eyes of Sqn Ldr Max Aitken, who is walking to the machine on the left, and Flt Lt Willie Rhodes-Moorhouse in white overalls on the right. The fighter on the right is UF-B.

Norman's first kill was a shared Junkers 88A like the one in the photograph, despatched on 15 August south of Spithead.

Brownings. Norman recorded several crewmen toppling into the water, either hit by his fire or attempting to evade it. During the latter part of April, he had a short posting to No.1 Aircraft Delivery Flight at Hendon, piloting a variety of machines to various localities in Britain. He reported ruefully on 5 May that he had been stopped for speeding when dashing from Kenley to Hendon by car! Norman was back with the Legion in late May, following them to Manston where they had been transferred.

On 25 May, Taylor had his first taste of aerial action since the heady days of 1940. Piloting Z3030 on an early morning Channel patrol in the Blue 2 slot, he picked out three duck-egg blue-green

Messerschmitt 110s to starboard at 500 feet just off Gravelines, which were unusual opponents to find operating by day at this time. The two-seaters were in a wide echelon to the left, and, turning to attack, Norman put a brief burst into the second adversary. There was no apparent result, and he swiftly pulled out to sea, sensing Blue 1 behind him. A quick glance showed it was not his companion, but a light camouflaged Me 109! A violent turn found the three *Zerstörers* on the inside of his curve, heading in the opposite direction. Taylor aimed a two-second burst from his twelve wing-guns into the leader, and was startled when his opponent abruptly plunged straight into the sea off Calais. He climbed sharply into a protecting cloud-mass overhead, orbiting for several minutes before emerging over the port above half-a-dozen Me 109s in line-astern below him. He took the heaven-sent opportunity to dive on the rearmost interceptor; a quick squeeze of the gun button and his tracers speared into the enemy fighter's wing, blowing away at least a fifth of the control surfaces. A large piece broke off, and the 109 staggered and rolled away in an inverted dive some 400 feet above the sea, its ailerons probably jammed. Norman slammed his throttle hard open, and the 1,200 horsepower of his straining Merlin pulled him away to safety, wave-hopping back across the Channel to England. Though he initially claimed a 110 destroyed and a 109 probable, the latter was elevated to a confirmed after further interrogation. In fact, a machine of 1/JG3 attempted a force-landing at nearby St Pol airfield around the time of the combat, crashing and killing its pilot.

The rest of May 1941 passed peacefully. In June, Taylor's considerable expertise was rewarded with the occasional leadership of the 'B' Flight, though he remained a lowly sergeant; indeed, his promotion to commissioned rank was long overdue. On 13 June he met the Luftwaffe again, with precisely the same results as before. He was flying Z2745 as Green 1, accompanied by Sergeant Mares as his number two on an afternoon Channel patrol 2 miles off Dover, when four black-painted, yellow-nosed Me 109s appeared head-on in a wide echelon to port at 3,000 feet. Norman identified them as 109Fs, the more powerful, cleaned-up successor to the Emil variant, as he locked on to the leader, spraying him with tracer. He saw black smoke gush away as his rounds penetrated the engine cowling. As the lean, long-nosed fighters flashed by, Taylor steep-turned to get on their tails, shifting his aim to the others, and managing a long burst as they swung round to the open sea. Two of the bandits dived vertically and he followed, his twelve Brownings spitting a continuous stream of fire. He pulled out at below a thousand feet as two further bogies appeared, but they were speedily lost in the haze. Green 2 had followed his leader and saw a widespreading white patch on the surface of the water where his number one's victims had crashed. Norman expended 1,800 rounds during this encounter, and Fighter Command HQ confirmed that two Messerschmitts had gone into the sea, hitting the water very close to each other.

Taylor's final action with 601 took place on 16 June. He was piloting Z2745 as Black 1 on a Channel sortie with FO Berg. Two Me 109s appeared, 12 miles off Dover, at 800 feet, and all four warplanes went into a fierce death-dance just above the waves. Norman took one of his opponents head-on, trading twelve machine guns for two cannon and two machine guns. He saw the muzzle-flashes as the Messerschmitt returned fire, and the tracer flitting over his canopy. His rounds struck both wing roots of his adversary, and for a heart-stopping second or two as they closed, he felt the inevitable end must be a violent fusion of Hurricane and 109, before the enemy fighter flashed overhead, so near that Z2745 rocked in its wake. He claimed a 'damaged', whilst his number two reported a probable for himself. In fact the pair may have done better than they thought. Two Me 109Es of 1/JG26 were reported lost in the locality on the 16th, and might well have been victims of Black Section. One Luftwaffe pilot was killed and the other rescued by the *Seenotdienst*.

Twenty-year-old Taylor's last operational flight with the Legion was an offensive sweep over the Channel in his long-serving Z2745, during which the Hurricanes escorted a Lysander flying at 500 feet. Perhaps as a mark of the esteem in which he was held, he led 'B' Flight on this sortie. During June he was awarded a well-merited Distinguished Flying Medal for taking part in 'numerous operational patrols' and for showing at all times 'great keenness and determination to engage the enemy'. He was also commissioned as a pilot officer. Doubtless wishing for more (or maybe a different sort of) action, he applied to join the Merchant Ship Fighter Unit (MSFU), and with a grand total of 461 flying hours, he reported to the war-battered port of Liverpool on 27 June to embark on the second phase of his RAF combat career.

The MSFU had been formed in early 1941 and set up at the old Liverpool civil airport at Speke on the River Mersey. It had been created to try and combat the extremely serious depredations of German long-range aircraft, which were attacking convoys and reporting their positions to U-boat packs in mid-Atlantic, an area then out of range of our own aircraft. The predominant threat was posed by the four-motor Focke-Wulf 200 Condor, flown by KG40 from airfields on the Atlantic seaboard. With an operational radius of 1,250 miles, these raiders were capable of sinking Allied merchantmen unaided.

Before the introduction of small 'Woolworth' aircraft carriers, the only practical antidote on offer was to adapt certain merchant vessels as 'Camships' – Catapult Armed Merchant Ships – with forward mounted ramps to rocket-launch Hurricane fighters to attack these predators in the remote fastnesses of these vital sea lanes. Dubbed 'Catafighters' or 'Hurricats', the combat-weary Mk I Hurricanes scheduled for use were considered expendable, and once launched the pilot and his charge were on a one-way trip, as few combats could be expected to occur within the range of land. Immediately his fuel was exhausted, the pilot baled out and trusted to a convoy escort to pick him up. It was exciting, if highly dangerous work, once a launching was authorised, but considerable boredom had to be endured, and many Catafighter pilots completed a number of voyages without ever seeing, let alone engaging, any enemy aircraft.

On 2 May 1941, Fighter Command issued a circular asking for 'officer volunteers who must be fully operational pilots' and described the hazardous and uncertain nature of the work. Norman presumably joined for the excitement, convinced that winning the Battle of the Atlantic was becoming as essential to his country's survival as the Battle of Britain had been nine months previously. As an individualist he may have jumped at the chance to be his own master, away from the restrictions of the squadron routine.

HEINKEL 111
shot down at
HUNSDON, HERTS.
August 30, 1940.
Salvaged by 334 S.L. Battery R.A.

Taylor's Blue Section Hurricanes shot down a Heinkel III at Hunsdon on 30 August. A piece of the bomber's wing is preserved in the Imperial War Museum, courtesy of 334 S.L. Battery RA. (Author)

On 31 August, Taylor destroyed an Me 109, though he was himself shot down by the German's No.2. Taylor, who was forced to bale out, had no idea that he had despatched the enemy fighter until told by the IO from the local airfield. The 109 crash-landed at Shornmead Fort, Gravesend, and the pilot, Fw. Kramer, was badly burned. Here, firemen, soldiers and civilians inspect the partially burnt-out wreckage. (Cornwell Collection)

Norman experienced his first catapult take-off, a ground launch that sent Fairey Fulmar N4079 hurtling across the airfield towards the Mersey on 28 June. Though useful for initiating pilots into the G-forces likely to be tolerated later, the Fulmar was far too slow for operational use, being little more than a re-jigged Battle with eight fixed wing-guns. Rocket-launches of Hurricanes commenced at Speke on 6 July, and Taylor experienced the 3.5g of his first 'bang-off', as they soon became known, in V7253 the following day. RDF radio-direction-finding and R/T trials at Belfast followed, which involved an intricate series of positioning flights between Abbotsinch, Speke, Bangor and Sydenham, and Belfast, with Norman frequently carrying full flying kit on and off trains and taxis to billets, airfields and the dock basin. While in Belfast he met his future wife, Florence Jean Miskimmen, to whom he proposed on 7 November, shortly before his first cruise on Camship *Empire Rowan*.

With Hurricane V7253 perched on its trolley astride the catapult rails, *Empire Rowan* set sail on the 14th, joining a convoy bound for Halifax, Nova Scotia. Once into the Atlantic the weather deteriorated, with the merchant vessel bucking into a heavy swell which sent corrosive salt-laden spray high over her bows. Seven days out from Belfast, large tears were found in the Hurricat's fuselage fabric. Driving snow, followed by freezing temperatures, cut short attempts at repairs, and high winds subsequently exacerbated the fabric damage. When Norman was able to inspect his machine again, he found out 'it was torn all over'.

After fourteen days at sea, Norman 'sighted Halifax and entered harbour. To see all the lights was great. We all had a drink and celebrated.' On Sunday Taylor's fighter was offloaded satisfactorily, but *Empire Rowan* lost her anchor at night and had to dock in 30 degrees of frost. A hospitable welcome awaited all Catafighter pilots and their Fighter Direction Officers (FDOs) at the Green Lantern in downtown Halifax, whose meals helped assuage the bitter December cold. On the following Sunday,

Above: *The Luftwaffe's scourge of the Atlantic was the Focke-Wulf 200C Condor, which had a vast range and could shadow Allied convoys in the mid-Atlantic.* (S. Ratledge)

Left: *601 sergeant pilots on readiness pose by a Hurricane during autumn 1940. Taylor is the tall figure at the rear. From left to right: Sgts Jensen, Hetherington and Weightman.* (S. Ratledge)

the 7th, Japanese carrier planes launched their unprovoked attack on Pearl Harbour. Norman noted: 'Britain and America at war with Japan. Blackout all down the West Coast.'

Repairs to the Hurricane's fabric were effected, and Norman was able to enjoy an hour's low flying from Dartmouth airfield on the 10th and 12th. On the latter date he dined in the Camship's already festive wardroom, and joined other members of the crew in going ashore 'to see *Keep 'Em Flying*, a very good picture. Supper, G.L.' The day before he had been out supervising a 'Rainbow' operation: the rocket-launching of a Hurricat, which was still a covert procedure, as the RCAF administration insisted that the technique was top secret and should not be seen by anyone! The freighter was loaded up with cargo for the return journey by Monday 15th, but conditions were too rough to mount the Hurricane and the intended convoy was missed. Wednesday dawned fine and Norman used the opportunity to supervise the servicing of the catapult trolley. Hurricane V7253 arrived on the same day, and by Saturday 20th the machine was safely locked on the catapult trolley, with all connections serviceable. Later that day Norman succumbed to a Clark Gable/Alice Faye film, and 'got on ship at 2 a.m. in a terrible blizzard.' The blizzard was still raging when *Empire Rowan* set sail from Halifax on the 21st on the homeward run.

The convoy steamed into driving snow, sleet, wind and endless rain. 'The boys were ill all day', Norman wrote in his diary, 'we're shipping water and their cabins are full of water. In the afternoon I managed to start the engine, ran quite well.' On Christmas Eve an American flying boat, bearing a large stars-and-stripes ensign, passed over the convoy and a telegram was received from the King. In the evening the aircrew threw a party, which the Convoy Commodore attended. By Boxing Day the gales had returned, with 'the sea splashing over the machine'. Despite being swept aft by a wave on the 28th, Norman spent the following day working on the Catafighter. 'Corrosion had got into the guns and ammunition, everything had to be taken out and greased.' The next day, nine days out from Halifax, was Norman's first 'readiness' as the convoy came within the FW 200 range. He was acutely disappointed that no order for an interception came, on that day or the remaining five.

On 5 January 1942, *Empire Rowan* and most of the convoy gained the relative sanctuary of Liverpool. Taylor was confined to Speke for the remainder of the winter, as the catapult fighters had taken a fearful battering from the seas. Despite spraying the aircraft interiors with lanolin resin, avalanches of spray had penetrated closed cockpits, corroding instruments and airframes. Storms had fractured control-locking gear, and gales had actually rotated the Hurricane airscrews against the compression of their Merlin's twelve cylinders. Captains had to forbid personnel from inspecting the catapults in the worse weather for days on end. MSFU actually curtailed the supply of Hurricanes to Camships on the North Atlantic run until the spring, trusting that the Luftwaffe's Condors would also be grounded in the worst weather.

Norman's log recorded interminable practice and test flights, including a force-landing on 9 March in Hurricane Z3665 at Mostyn, but his break came on 14 May when he joined *Empire Gale* on the Gibraltar run, which was an uneventful voyage with Hurricane V6927 left perched on her catapult trolley. From June to October he served with the MSFU detachment on the Rock, savouring the equable climate and the luxuries to the full. He flew several of the unit's Hurricanes on practices, patrols, reconnaissances and air tests. Excitement was rare; sometimes he flew along the Spanish and Moroccan coasts, occasionally coming under inaccurate anti-aircraft fire. He went in search of reported Junkers 52 transports twice and once chased a Heinkel III, but was doubtless very pleased when he joined the Camship *Empire Heath,* which sailed on 25 October in a home-bound convoy of sixty-five ships, carrying the Sea Hurricane V7070 on her catapult.

Gibraltar convoys had their landward flank exposed to enemy airfields for their entire outward and homebound voyages, particularly KG 40's Condor base at Bordeaux-Merignac, to the west of the city. Just before 10 a.m. on the bright, clear morning of 1 November, with the convoy some 250 miles off the Spanish coast, an air attack warning was hoisted by the convoy commodore. It was impractical to route Gibraltar convoys beyond the Condor's operational radius of 1,250 miles;

Norman's convoy was well out into the Atlantic, proceeding north on 15 degrees west, but not more than 700 flying miles from Bordeaux.

Nothing was seen from the monkey island above the bridge for an hour, when a low-flying aircraft appeared some 8 miles away, ahead of the convoy and approaching from landwards. 'Action Stations' alarm bells clanged throughout the ship immediately. Norman and his FDO officer, Sub-Lieutenant S.L. 'Ginger' Ward, identified the aircraft as a Condor, which was flying too low to show up on radar screens. Taylor rushed forward, climbed the Hurricat's wing and settled into the cockpit, donning his helmet and tightly strapping himself in. As he started the motor and went through his pre-flight checks, his reserve pilot, P.D. 'Paddy' O'Sullivan, raced to the steel firing hut in the forepeak to take the trolley's safety locking-bolt keep-pins from the sea-crew corporal.

The FW 200 was now turning to fly parallel to the convoy, maintaining its eight-mile distance. 'Ginger' Ward, up on the monkey island and responsible for launching the Hurricane, was becoming increasingly uncertain of the Condor's intentions. He decided to scrub the shoot, partly to avoid overheating the Merlin engine, giving the Catapult Firing Officer (CFO) O'Sullivan the switch-off signal, who relayed it to Taylor. Comparative peace was restored. The Condor continued to stalk the convoy, commencing a second turn to port at a discreet distance astern and, almost immediately, the multi-engined raider tightened the turn, banking round to line up on a specifically selected target – *Empire Heath* herself. To the Condor captain, she was an apparent straggler steaming out on the convoy's vulnerable flank and away to the rear (to give her Hurricane maximum sea space for launching). Over the R/T, Ward ordered Taylor to restart his engine, and the ship's helm was put over to starboard into the wind to give the Catafighter a perfect take-off.

With the menacing shape of the Focke-Wulf approaching from dead astern 4 miles away, Sub-Lt Ward ordered the launch. O'Sullivan plugged in the safety link and raised his blue flag to inform Captain Hammett that the aircraft was ready for launching. A second ringing of the klaxon warned the ship's crew to take cover from the imminent rocket blast. The Master displayed his blue flag for O'Sullivan to launch as soon as he was ready, whereupon he rotated his flag for the pilot to fully open his throttle. The Hurricane, still rigidly tethered to its cradle, vibrated as though it was possessed and yearning for release.

Taylor raised his right arm, waiting for the bows of the Camship to lift with the swell, before giving the signal to fire the fourteen three-inch diameter rockets and send the Hurricat accelerating along its 69-foot journey on the trolley. His preparations were complete; throttle nut tightened, one-third flaps, one-third starboard rudder to cancel out the fighter's incipient swing to the left, elevators and trim tabs central, and left elbow firmly forced into the hip to prevent the control column being drawn back too sharply. The stick had to be eased back gently or the aeroplane could easily stall into the sea. Norman jammed his head hard into the heavily-padded rest to absorb the velocity, and just as the bows lifted almost to the horizontal, he cut down his arm abruptly. O'Sullivan, almost deafened by the engine noise, pulled, then rotated, the firing switch, igniting the rockets with a deafening roar and a blinding coruscation of light. The steel restraining strop sheared, and the grey-green Catafighter hurtled along on its cradle, accelerating seemingly instantly to 80mph. Norman felt his face distort under 3.5g pressure, jowls flattening against his cheekbones. O'Sullivan instinctively ducked as the fighter's starboard wing skimmed his firing hut in the forepeak, and the now-empty trolley slammed into the hydraulic buffers just above him.

As clouds of acrid smoke from the spent rockets swirled aft over *Empire Heath*'s superstructure, Norman raised the flaps, slid his canopy shut, switched on IFF and, testing his R/T, banked round in a wide turn to port, back over the ship. The R/T frequency was obliterated by jamming, probably emanating from the Condor itself. The bright sun, glinting hard off the sea, impeded his vision, and he had to know where his opponent was. Roaring back over the Camship, he saw the pointing arms of the crew waving south-west in the direction of the Condor, which had swung away low over the water as soon as the enemy aircrew had noticed V7070's remarkable launching pyrotechnics. The four-engined raider headed directly into the sun to make detection doubly difficult. Knowing the

Taylor's Sea Hurricane IA V6927 sits expectantly on Empire Gale's *catapult trolley, outward bound in convoy on the Liverpool-Gibraltar run in May 1942.* (S. Ratledge)

The uninviting pilot's-eye view of the incredibly short catapult ramp, necessitating a force of 3.5g at take-off. (S. Ratledge)

Taylor and fellow pilot Joe Lamb perch on Hurricat V6927 *mounted on* Empire Gale's *fo'c'sle catapult. The LU code identifies it as a pool-unit aircraft for the MSFU.* (S. Ratledge)

Empire Heath *heads home from Gibraltar in late October 1942, with Sea Hurricane V7070 on its catapult ramp. This excellent study shows the details of the catapult trolley and launching rail to perfection.* (S. Ratledge)

Taylor sits on V6927's cowling aboard Empire Gale *on the passage to Gibraltar in May 1942.* (S. Ratledge)

250 miles west of Spain, V7070 perches expectantly on its cradle just a few hours before its combat with a KG40 Condor. Note that the ramp is offset to prevent flames and smoke from the blast-off from damaging the bridge, and also to ensure that in the event of a mislaunch the ship did not run down a ditched pilot. (S. Ratledge)

A fine shot of one of the sinister Condors shows the two dorsal turrets which deployed a heavy armament. There was another gun-carrying gondola under the fuselage, which is visible in the top picture on p.40.

high skills of the KG 40 long-range fliers, Taylor guessed their tactics, and, snarling along at full boost, 2,600 revs a minute and approaching 300 mph, he picked out the silhouette of the Axis aircraft some 6 miles up-sun.

Norman gained rapidly on the heavily-armed FW 200, admiring its sinister elegance, the streamlined fuselage, slender wings and stately empennage which betrayed the raider's civilian pedigree. Still troubled by the glare from the sea, he rattled off a short burst ahead of the German in an attempt to force him round and to avoid staring into the intense sunlight. As he closed, the enemy gunners began hosing him with tracer from several positions. The Focke-Wulf increased speed, and Taylor had to pull the boost override to keep up. This was V7070's final trip, and the strain on the over-revving Merlin was immaterial. He had to ease back from the full twelve pounds boost pressure to a more moderate nine, as a slight coolant leak sprayed glycol on his windscreen.

Closing on the dull-sea-grey bomber from starboard and above, he endured blistering streams of tracer from the forward dorsal turret and a starboard beam gun. Through continuous defensive fire he crossed the Condor's tail, ripping off a four-second burst from 150 yards, then sliding away to port. He did not escape unscathed. A return burst slashed through his port wing, with one bullet emerging from the dead centre of the red and blue roundel. Taylor's concentration was so absolute that he had no idea he had been hit. He hung on above and to port of his adversary, awaiting the next move. Anxious to avoid his tenacious opponent, the German pilot headed for a layer of cloud at 1,200 feet, rising like a lift as he opened the throttles of his four growling Bramo Fafnir nine-cylinder radials for the climb. It was a fatal mistake; as it nosed upwards, the raider had to pass straight through the MSFU pilot's GM2 gunsight. At 300 feet and only 200 yards away, Taylor only needed minimum deflection as the grey Condor drifted through the luminous orange ring of his reflector. A three-second stream of .303 inch tracer, directed with deadly accuracy, tore into the vulnerable cockpit area, flailing the enclosed space with lead and riddling the pilot. As he died he dragged back on the control column, and the huge machine, its 108-foot wingspan looking enormous as it reared above the Hurricane, began a steep climb, with the uninjured gunners still ripping off bursts of withering fire which snaked around Taylor as he followed. The English pilot was unaware that he had dealt the Focke-Wulf a mortal blow. He thought the sudden climb was a clever ploy, especially as his quarry abruptly stalled away, plunging towards the ocean in a shallow dive, intent on resuming, to Norman, his wave-hopping routine to frustrate the defender into a further wastage of ammunition and petrol.

Wrong-footed by the unexpected dive, Norman lost ground, pulling his straining fighter round to follow. He looked on, astounded, as the Condor failed to ease out and smashed with alarming suddenness into the slate-grey sea. Great curtains of spray rose up, hiding the doomed giant. When the boiling water subsided, only the tailplane and great squared-off swastika-decorated fin and rudder remained, sticking up like a marker to indicate its position. Taylor jubilantly screamed his success over the R/T as he orbited the wreckage in the unlikely event that some of the crew had survived the impact. The projecting empennage slid beneath the waves, and only a wide patch of fluorescent marker dye remained to locate where seven men had died.

Thirty-seven years on, Norman receives the supreme accolade as the hero on the front page of the Victor *comic!*

Norman was now over 40 miles away from the convoy. He climbed to 2,000 feet, away from the sun, and managed to contact his FDO, Ward, on the radio. Ward gave him a vector to steer, and at midday he had the convoy in sight. Still exhilarated, he came low over the mastheads, completing a succession of slow rolls to announce his victory. *Empire Heath* virtually manned the side for him, the crew dancing and cheering on deck, whilst the 'whoop-whoop' of sirens echoed over the water as every vessel saluted his feat. Only on the third victory roll did he notice the bullet-strikes on his port wing and ease off the aerobatics. Resuming his status as reserve pilot, 'Paddy' O'Sullivan questioned Norman closely on the R/T, asking for precise details of the action, as not all Catapilots survived their bale-outs, and important lessons might be learned from his combat tactics and those of his adversary. Ward ensured that the pick-up vessel, the Flower-class corvette HMS *Sweet Briar*, was on station, and ordered his pilot to jump.

Aiming to hit the sea just ahead of the warship, Norman jettisoned his cockpit canopy and emergency panel, unbuckled his safety straps, and worked his feet to the right of the control column. He throttled back to 150mph, trimmed the warplane slightly tail-heavy, crouched, and thrusting himself head-first out of the cockpit, cleared the trailing edge of the starboard wing. Once clear of the tailplane, he worked the D-ring of his parachute. The canopy opened with a jerk, and he watched with some regret as his faithful V7070, who had done all that was asked of her, dropped her port wing and glided into the Atlantic in a graceful curve.

Unfortunately Taylor had twisted his harness on the jump, and during his ninety-second descent could not control his fall. He hit the sea hard, on his back, and managed to release the dragging canopy. A non-swimmer, he kicked off his flying boots and struggled to inflate his lifejacket. The seal on his air bottle stubbornly refused to break, and though able he was able to keep afloat, his legs became entangled in the waterlogged parachute, whilst the small dinghy behind his back was likewise caught up in the shroud lines. After surviving the dangerous combat, Norman was possessed with the despairing thought that he was going to drown at the end of it.

Struggling violently to clear his dinghy, he rapidly exhausted himself, swallowing copious draughts of seawater. Barely able to keep afloat, and sinking 'for the thirty-third time' under the impetus of a huge wave, he glimpsed a lifebelt ahead. He reached and clung on gratefully, unaware that the wave was caused by the blunt, thrusting bows of HMS *Sweet Briar*. The lifebelt was still attached to the corvette, and the hapless pilot was taken under involuntary tow until the line mercifully broke. He lay wallowing desperately, till strong hands dragged his soaked and spent body into a boat. At 12.30 p.m., wrapped in a warm blanket, Norman was handed aboard the corvette and treated to a welcome dose of Navy rum. A hot bath, dry clothes and further tots restored his equilibrium, and by 3.50 p.m. he was returned to his own ship. In his logbook he recorded spending twenty minutes 'in the Drink'. His advice to future intrepid Catapilots was 'Take my tip and learn to swim.'

During Norman's sojourn at Gibraltar, the training of MSFU pilots in bale-out procedures had become more thorough, and now comprised a ten-day course at the Parachute Training School at Ringway. It culminated in a live drop into Tatton Park Lake. Norman had failed to inform his MSFU selection board that he was a non-swimmer, as no one had bothered to ask him! The reward for his exploit was swift and justified – an immediate Distinguished Flying Cross. Both the AOC 9 Group and C-in-C Western Approaches sent congratulatory telegrams, with the former adding 'Well done, MSFU.' The award, gazetted in December, paid tribute to the pilot's great skill in the desperate combat, adding that 'His courageous and skilful work earned the admiration of officers of the ships in the convoy who witnessed the operation.' Thirty-seven years later, Norman Taylor DFC DFM received the ultimate accolade when his feat was told in pictorial form on the cover of the *Victor* comic, issue 971!

The convoy reached England on 8 November, with the Derbyshire flier earning a well-deserved rest, followed by a quiet spell at Speke. He stayed with the MSFU, adding drogue-towing and ADDLs – Aerodrome Dummy Deck Landings – on HMS *Argus* to his aerial repertoire. It was a

Left: *Norman, wearing the ribbons of both his decorations, relaxes with an archetypal-looking pilot known only as 'Smithy'.* (S. Ratledge) Right: *Norman Taylor's tombstone at Gutersloh proudly designates him as 'One of the Few'.* (S. Ratledge)

useful skill now that Sea Hurricanes could expect to land on the new, small escort carriers and thus live to fight another day. Norman left the MSFU in April 1943, with an accumulated 683 flying hours to his credit, earning an 'Above Average' assessment in every category of flying skill. During the winter he had managed the occasional flight to Belfast, and at the end of April he married his fiancée, Jean, at Fortwilliam Church. A son, Rowan, was born in 1944, and a daughter, Sallie, in 1948, five months after his death.

Supported by Gp Capt George Pinkerton, CO of the MSFU, Norman had applied for flying duties within the RAF, and in September 1943 returned to his native county. He took up a posting to Rolls-Royce Ltd in Derby, where he alternated flying sessions from Hucknall with instructing RAF and Fleet Air Arm personnel at the Aero Engine School on Victory Road. When he was promoted to flight lieutenant, with a well-earned Air Efficiency Award, he instilled in his student pilots and flight engineers an 'owner-driver' attitude to engine handling, particularly regarding the improvement of endurance and operating radius. He test-flew Merlin-powered Mustangs extensively in 1944 to establish long-range operating criteria, and later piloted his first jet fighter, the Meteor III. This unusual posting came to an end in late November 1945, when his flying hours had risen to a grand total of 961. In December he was posted to 245 Squadron at Colerne, flying Meteors. He progressed to 222, another Meteor unit, at Exeter in February 1946, as OC 'B' Flight. In April he completed 1,000 flying hours, and on 9 May he participated in the Victory anniversary flypast over Jersey and Guernsey, piloting Meteor EE447. For the even more prestigious flypast over London on 8 June, he flew EE420, operating at 350mph in appalling weather. The Meteors gave 'a superb example of perfect formation flying'.

In July 1947, before a posting to 33 Squadron, Norman was part of the RAF escort to the battleship HMS *Vanguard,* carrying the Royal Family from Portsmouth on an official tour to South Africa. His sojourn with 33, who flew Tempest IIs from Fassberg, West Germany, was only short.

In October he commenced an instrument weather-rating instructor's course at the Empire Flying School, bumbling around in Oxfords and Harvards. By December his logbooks showed he had piloted a plethora of additional aircraft types. In a significant measure, Norman's expressed boyhood ambition of test flying was being fully realised.

His sister Eva once reflected that:

> ... if there was anything that wanted doing, Norman would do it. He didn't know the meaning of fear, and just lived for the day. His flair for devilment led him into countless scrapes as a boy; hanging from the girders of a favourite railway bridge while the crack St Pancras to Manchester express thundered overhead, and cycling along its parapet from end to end were two that come to mind.

Caught in a torrential storm whilst camping out for the night with school chum Arthur Jackson, the pair of ten-year-olds decided to dash for home with their saturated tent held high over their heads. This apparition stampeded a grey shire horse into bolting round its field, and the unfortunate beast eventually expired from its exertions.

Many years later, Norman's parents returned to Derbyshire, but once home on leave, Norman would be impatient to forsake Allestree's Gisborne Crescent and motorcycle to Melbourne. There he would spend a day working the draught horses, or scarifying a few acres of his ex-schoolfriends' market gardens. His final move, in January 1948, was to the Station Flight, 135 Wing, RAF Gutersloh, commanded by the famous fighter pilot Frank Carey. At Gutersloh, Norman flew Harvards on instrument rating tests, doubtless feeling this was a vastly different proposition to the fast jets he had become used to during the past few years. On 29 April, three weeks after Jean had joined him and one day before their fifth wedding anniversary, he took off in Harvard IIB KF569. A short time later, near Wunsdorf, west of Hanover, the aircraft lost power on approach and spun into the ground, killing both occupants.

Norman Taylor had taken all the enemy could throw at him in concentrated periods through 1940 and 1941, and had subsequently survived the nearest thing to a kamikaze operation mounted by the RAF during the Second World War. It is poignant that death came, as it did for so many fine Derbyshire pilots, not as a result of enemy action, but in a flying accident, that was not even in wartime, but in the palmy days of peace. Norman Taylor was only twenty-seven at the time of his death and lies buried at Gutersloh. His neat official tombstone bears the words he was most likely to have approved, designating him proudly as 'One of the Few'. No fighter pilot could wish for a better epitaph.

three

Air Commodore
Philip James Sanders
DFC

Combat Record

Date	Sqn	Locality	Aircraft Flown	Enemy Type	Claim
02.06.40	92	Dunkirk	Spitfire I N3285	Heinkel III	Destroyed
				Heinkel III	Probable
09.09.40	92	S.E. Biggin Hill	Spitfire I R6624	Heinkel III	Destroyed
		Dungeness		Messerschmitt 109E	Probable
11.09.40	92	Dungeness	Spitfire I R6624	Heinkel III	Destroyed
		N. of Tonbridge		Messerschmitt 109E	Destroyed
		Dover		Messerschmitt 109E	Probable
15.09.40	92	Maidstone	Spitfire I X4051	Dornier 17Z	Destroyed
20.09.40	92	Dymchurch	Spitfire I X4418	Messerschmitt 109E	Destroyed

A charcoal portrait of Squadron Leader Philip James Sanders DFC, by Sir William Rothenstein. (P.J. Sanders)

Air Commodore Philip James Sanders DFC

PHILIP SANDERS, who was born in Chesterfield in 1911, became the highest-ranking Derbyshire fighter pilot of the post-Second World War period. He was also the forgotten man as far as the annals of 92 Squadron, the unit he commanded in 1940, are concerned. He has been the subject of much misrepresentation and uninformed comment, almost to the extent of achieving invisibility. Researchers who have been less than thorough have ignored his very real achievements as CO of the squadron during the Battle of Britain, and some have managed the seemingly impossible, having written histories of the unit and its star pilots without bothering to mention him once! A leader credited with six enemy aircraft destroyed, plus a DFC, can hardly qualify for the title of the man who never was; yet some who should know better have totally overlooked his contribution to the success of 92, a controversial and high-profile element of Fighter Command during the first full year of the war.

Philip Sanders was born at Somersall Hall in May 1911, which was a fine house, just a tram ride away from the nearby Brampton terminus to Chesterfield town centre. He was the youngest and of the seven children born to his parents, Florence and Henry, the sole survivor until his death in January 1989. His father was a successful solicitor who came to Derbyshire in the 1890s to head the partnership of Davies, Sanders and Swanwick. Philip was educated at Cheltenham and Balliol College, Oxford. He graduated, as a matter of course, in law, with the intention of qualifying as a solicitor himself and joining the family firm, but his father's death in 1933 left him in a quandary. Though he commenced articles in the City, he realised he was not cut out for the profession. Finding that he was eligible for a permanent RAF commission as a university graduate, he applied to join the Service and was accepted in December 1935.

He found life at No.5 Flying Training School in Sealand most enjoyable, training on Tiger Moths and Hawker Furies, and emerging with a Distinguished Pass rating. His first operational posting was to No.1 Squadron at Tangmere in mid-1936, where he overlapped with two other Derbyshire-born stalwarts, PO Lawrie Henstock and later Sergeant Arthur Clowes. Philip became a flight commander in early 1939, remaining at Tangmere long enough to see his unit re-equip with Hurricanes and the arrival of 'Bull' Halahan. He was anxious to point out to me that he, and not the Bull, as some writers have stated, led No.1 in a beat-up of Tangmere on Empire Air Day in July 1939. Halahan, having not long arrived, delegated this task to Sanders, who led fifteen Hurricanes in a low, close-formation diving pass over the airfield in warplane NA-G.

In August 1939 Philip was posted as Sector Operations Officer and Fighter Controller at Hornchurch. In September he married his Dutch fiancée, Maria Welbergen, the daughter of the Swiss head of Shell petroleum. He enjoyed, as he put it, 'quite unexpectedly, a little married life before the storm broke.' The German *Blitzkrieg* of May 1940, and the subsequent evacuation of the BEF from Dunkirk, led to casualties among the RAF fighters covering the rescue operations. Sanders was earmarked as a replacement for Roger Bushell, CO of 92, who had been shot down and captured. The energetic and forthright Bushell was the mastermind of many RAF escapes from the German concentration camps, and he was eventually murdered by the Gestapo in March 1944 after the Great Escape from Stalag Luft III.

Courtesy of the Hornchurch squadron commanders, there was just enough time for Sanders to snatch a few hours' practice on Spitfire Mk Is, to get his hand in before transferring to Northolt on 25 May to lead a unit which had only been in existence for eight months. 92 had been created from a nucleus of 601 Squadron, and its philosophy and outlook had been shaped by its first CO. There was little time for Sanders or the pilots now under him to take stock of each other. The Dunkirk evacuation was in full swing, and early on the morning of 2 June his command, operating temporarily from Martlesham as part of a wing including 32, 266 and 611 Squadrons, took off for a sweep of the Calais-Dunkirk area. It must be stressed that Sanders was no tyro, having flown modern interceptors with

No.1, but in view of his total lack of operational experience, which was certainly not his fault, he sensibly opted to put Flt Lt Robert S. Tuck as combat leader, whilst he led Green Section in support.

The formidable air armada swept on towards Dunkirk, 32 Squadron with its lower-performance Hurricanes acting, perhaps inappropriately, as top-cover at 23,000 feet, which was not their best operating height. The Spitfires of 266 flew below them, whilst 92 patrolled the lowest level, some 14,000 feet above the sea. The weather was dull with heavy layers of thin cloud up to 25,000 feet, and there was a thick haze of smoke all around the port. At 8 a.m. a formation of some thirty Heinkel IIIH-2s from KG54 were sighted flying several thousand feet below 92, and Tuck led Blue Section into the attack.

As they approached, Sanders, obviously tense at his initial clash with the enemy, led Green Section against a sub-formation of the German bombers in Spitfire N3285. The gaggle of six raiders were in two vics of three, with the second section astern and slightly to port of the leading one. Sanders' trio of Spitfires, 1,500 feet above and behind their targets, waited whilst Tuck's section engaged; he then ordered line-astern and rapidly closed with the rear vic, noting the standard mid-and-dark green splinter camouflage on the sinister-looking machines, whose black fuselage crosses were painted over yellow roundels. He lined up the right-hand aircraft in the orange circle of his illuminated gunsight, opening fire at 250 yards and aiming three short bursts as he closed to one hundred, breaking away to repeat the attack. Under fire from his section the three bombers had spread out, denying themselves the mutual protection of their defensive armament. Sanders closed to within one hundred yards of his original quarry, and his multiple Brownings rattled off a four-second burst which struck the starboard wing of the raider. A large piece broke away from the trailing edge and fluttered past him, evidently the right aileron. A warning of enemy fighters sounded in his earphones and he broke away rapidly. Confirming that the immediate area was clear of 109s, he was unable to locate his victim, or indeed any of the section his Spitfires had attacked. Ahead was another vic of Heinkel IIIH-2s who had turned through 180 degrees to port and were heading in the opposite direction.

Again Sanders selected the right-hand bomber, approaching for a starboard quarter attack from 200 down to some seventy-five yards – practically point-blank range. Under his concentrated fire, the aircraft's starboard Jumo burst into flames and began disgorging a thickening scarf of black smoke. Some of the squadron leader's rounds pierced the hydraulic system, causing the undercarriage wheels to swing down, adding their deadening drag to the difficulties of handling the stricken aircraft, which slowly broke formation in a spiral to the right. 'I did not observe the E/A crash', he wrote in his combat report, 'but it was clearly completely disabled'. The rest of the unit pulverised the other targets, claiming a total of fourteen, plus four Me 109 escorts. This was later amended to eleven, plus two 109s. Sanders was given credit for one Heinkel destroyed and one probable. These were his first victories.

Brought up on the uncompromising and firm hand of Roger Bushell, the old hands of 92 found Sanders a very different proposition. The late Tony Bartley, a stalwart of the unit, thought him 'a very nice fellow, but to us hooligans, not our type at all'. In his *Smoke Trails in the Sky*, he recalled 'Judy' Sanders, as he was apparently nicknamed, as being 'the complete antithesis of Roger, with no combat experience, which wasn't his fault. Poor devil, to take on us lot.' Lauded by Fighter Command, with morale high due to their substantial victories, Bartley felt that 92 'just couldn't respect any other leaders than those we had: Roger Bushell and Bob Tuck. We were a bolshie bunch of bastards, our tails riding high.' Another commentator confirmed 'it is clear that Sanders, though by no means an ineffective or unpopular officer, found it difficult to establish his position as the new leader of 92 Squadron.'

It is certain that they were no easy ride for a CO who had yet to prove himself. They had a notorious reputation for their contemptuous attitude towards the normal conventions of Service discipline, which included driving high-powered cars, sporting unconventional dress and indulging in wild parties – all part of the Auxiliary tradition fostered by Bushell. On consideration perhaps only an experienced leader, in tune with this spirit, could hope to establish early authority over this mettlesome team. As they covered themselves with glory over Dunkirk, their attitude towards

In this view of No.1 Squadron at the time of Munich, Sanders is standing in front of the rudder of the *Hawker Fury*, with Darky Clowes on his left. In front of the pair of Derbyshire fliers is Billy Drake, who was later to score over twenty kills with the RAF. (Squadron Archives)

Sanders, in Hurricane NA-G, leads out the squadron for a beat-up of Tangmere on Empire Air Day in July 1939. (P.J. Sanders)

Sanders met Heinkel IIIs, like the one depicted here, on several occasions while leading 92 Squadron. In fact, three of his confirmed victories were scored against aircraft of this type, including one over Dunkirk.

Philip also clashed with Messerschmitt 109Es on patrol, shooting down two of the single-seaters in combat. (Author)

authority became even worse. It is to Sanders' credit that he persevered and steadily gained the experience necessary to take full command.

Bob Tuck was instrumental in posting in Flt Lt Brian Kingcome from 65 Squadron to take over 'A' Flight, and the legend has grown that whenever 92 went into action, either he or the latter led the outfit, with Sanders presumably hanging on somewhere behind. Many accounts accept this arrangement as *de facto,* and produce factional R/T conversations in support of this contention. From the start of Sanders' takeover, this legend begins. On 16 June a section of Spitfires from 92 flew a reconnaissance patrol over France. One highly-spiced account credited Tuck with leading three fighters who seem to have conducted a private war, strafing anti-aircraft gun posts and a whole German motorised column. A magazine article published in 1988 perpetuated this myth, whilst reducing the number of participating Spitfires to two, again led by Tuck. This was written despite the fact that the squadron diary clearly shows four aircraft took part, led by Sanders flying R6624. They patrolled Abbeville-Amiens-Doulon, and during the sortie accurate light flak blew away part of Tuck's starboard wingtip. In retaliation Sanders recalled a beat-up of some German flak positions, but did not remember an assault on an army convoy.

Philip realised he had taken over 'a young, spirited, well-trained squadron' and, though admitting that his stewardship of 92 was 'no joyride', he paid tribute and told of his own undying 'admiration for the courage, devotion and incredible morale of the young pilots I was privileged to lead ... they did a great deal of damage to the Luftwaffe, but they paid a high price.'

On 18 June the squadron, then in 10 Group and tasked with the defence of Bristol, was moved from the front line to the backwater of Pembrey, near Kidwelly, on the South Wales coast. They took the move badly, though it seems clear that the sprightly team were simply being rested and given the chance to re-form, adjust to a new CO, and train up a fresh injection of pilots to replace the Dunkirk casualties. 92 started badly by beating up the tranquil Celtic countryside and arousing the wholesale ire of a locality as yet untouched by the realities of war. Bartley put up an early black by having to force-land when his Merlin cut out during a long slow-roll. He mistook a bog for a field, and on struggling to *terra firma* plastered in mud, was arrested by the Local Defence Volunteers as a spy – hardly surprising as he was attired in red trousers and sported an Old Stoic tie! Sanders was hauled before the station commander and warned that such antics were increasing the unpopularity of fighter pilots, who were still being unfairly blamed for their supposed inaction during the Dunkirk evacuation.

Despite the current of misinformation to the contrary, Sanders was no passenger during the waiting period before the breaking of the expected storm. He continued the training programme and took steps to keep in touch with tactics in the main battle area by detaching pilots for short periods to prepare them for what was to come. In mid-August 'A' Flight was moved to Bibury in Gloucestershire and experienced a taste of night patrols. This, at a time when the 11 Group squadrons were in the thick of the first phase of the Battle, was hard to take, though it was not to last for long. In early September AVM Keith Park, AOC 11 Group, decided to concentrate his Spitfire squadrons at Biggin Hill and Hornchurch, giving the interceptors a chance of hitting the enemy on their way to London.

92 Squadron were moved to the Bump on the 8th, to be joined four days later by 72 Squadron who arrived from Croydon. Among the latter unit's pilots was another Derbyshire flier, Sergeant Pilot Norman 'Sticky' Glew, who was also destined to make his mark in campaigns to come. Biggin Hill had suffered severely from Luftwaffe attacks, though by the time 92 were settling in these had abated, as the Germans shifted tactics and embarked on large-scale raids on the capital. Sanders led his command into action from the Bump for the first time on the 9th. His combat report clearly shows that by this time he was in his rightful place as Gannic Blue Leader, piloting R6624, and not as subordinate to Brian Kingcome or anyone else. By this time, Bob Tuck had been posted to lead 257 Squadron, which was another unit that needed some whipping into shape, though in their case the problem was not a high conceit of themselves, but a singular lack of combat success. At 5 p.m. 92 were patrolling Dungeness at 26,000 feet when the R/T crackled an urgent warning of 'snappers' – predatory Messerschmitt 109s coming down from above. Sanders' flight broke hard to port as Green Section were attacked behind them, and the CO was just in time to release a quick burst at a 109 as it pulled away from the section, also heading left. In trying to get a bead on his opponent, he turned too tightly and spun out.

92 Squadron spent some time in the summer of 1940 in the backwater of Pembrey in South Wales. This picture shows two of the unit's Spitfires, with a Blenheim I in the background. (P.J. Sanders)

Regaining control, Sanders found Blue 2 had stuck with him. Control ordered a return to base, giving a warning of bandits in the vicinity. At an altitude of 13,000, feet a formation of Heinkel IIIs were sighted in close vics some 10 miles S.S.E. of Biggin Hill, heading directly towards Sanders and his wingman. The CO had time to line up a bomber on the left-hand side of the shoal, loosing off four second's worth of concentrated fire as he closed head-on to within a hundred yards of his quarry. He broke upwards, skimming over his opponent and, turning hard to starboard, saw the Heinkel drift out of position, going down in a left-hand turn. The Me 109 escort soon put in an appearance, and Philip was joined by a yellow-nosed Messerschmitt with a yellow patch on the front of its fuselage, which was perhaps a unit badge. The pair circled warily before he used R6624's tighter turning radius to get inside his antagonist and loose off a deflection shot. The 109 immediately half-rolled and plunged away (which were standard evasion tactics), using his fighter's quicker initial dive, emitting black smoke – perhaps from the exhausts – as he engaged full boost from his Diamler-Benz motor. Sanders was quick to follow, snapping off several short bursts as, straining hard, he closed on his adversary to within 200 yards. Unfortunately low-lying clouds were by this time quite near, and the Messerschmitt was safely swallowed up in a thick layer at 8,000 feet.

Having expended some 1,750 rounds of ammunition, Sanders returned to base, claiming a Heinkel III destroyed and an Me 109 probable. The claims, unless they had the benefit of independent corroboration, seem inflated, and perhaps the III as a probable and the 109 a damaged would seem more appropriate on the evidence of his own report.

Two days later the Derbyshire flier led 92 into action again in R6624. They were vectored on to a large concentration of Heinkel IIIs, probably from KG26, with 109 escorts above, crossing the coast in the vicinity of Dungeness at Angels 20 at around 4 p.m. Sanders led the attack from above and abeam, singling out a target on the right-hand side of the mass and closing to within one hundred yards to deliver a long and telling burst. The cone of fire from his eight wing-guns set the raider's starboard engine on fire; flames blew backwards and the motor began trailing a long streamer of thick black smoke as the Spitfire veered away. The attack had taken the Germans and their pursuers across Kent, and a short time later, prowling north of Tonbridge, he picked out the shark-like shape of a 109 skimming low over the fields, heading south for France. Sanders came down on the unsuspecting enemy pilot from above, framing the Messerschmitt in a no-deflection shot in the luminous ring of his reflector. He saw his tracer striking home at close range, and following two short bursts the 109 hit the ground, its ruptured fuel tanks setting the wreckage ablaze. His most likely victim was a 109E-7, Wn 2029 of 1/LG2, which crashed near the Pilgrim's Way, Wrotham Hill, at around 4.14 p.m., killing its pilot, Uffz. Heckmaier. The London Air Museum later excavated the crash site, recovering sections of the shattered airframe. During both actions, Sanders expended some 2000 rounds of ammunition.

After refuelling at the Bump, he led his unit on an early evening patrol between Ashford and Ramsgate at 16,000 feet. Near Dover at 6 p.m., the pilots noticed condensation trails marking the skies at 20,000 feet, and climbed hard to investigate. Sanders described the warplanes making the trails as 'snappers'. He manoeuvred himself below and to port of one unheeding *Emil* and thumbed off a deflection shot from behind. His tracer went rapidly home, the unfortunate Messerschmitt absorbing the greater part of 500 rounds, half-rolling lazily to the right and dragging a trail of grey-black smoke as it dived out of sight. The presence of other German fighters above prevented the canny Sanders from following his hard-hit victim down. His claims for the day included one Heinkel III and one Messerschmitt 109 destroyed, with a further 109 probable. The squadron leader was certainly proving himself in the best, in indeed the only, way he could by leading his men into the thick of the battle and by building up his own combat claims, which now stood at four confirmed and two probables. He recalled that at Biggin Hill:

> ... we enjoyed early successes but at heavy cost until we learned how to cope with the high or close escorts, and how to re-form at least into pairs after the first engagement. The transition from a milling mass to an empty sky would be very sudden.

Two of the squadron's Spitfires, QJ-D and QJ-Y, warm up at Biggin Hill before setting off on an operational patrol in September 1940. (P.J. Sanders)

On 15 September, Sanders claimed a Dornier 17Z, which he shot down near Maidstone. It was like the one shown here.

A section of three Spitfires of 92 Squadron await the scramble call during the Battle of Britain. (P.J. Sanders)

Of 15 September, Battle of Britain Day, he had:

> ... *a clear memory, the day when everything went right. Our first interception was a big formation of Do 17s whose escorts had likely been diverted or had lost their way. 92 and our neighbouring squadron largely formed up again and continued the engagement as the enemy formation loosened. It was, in fact, a climax of the battle, although not the end of it.*

After action in the late morning, when Kingcome might well have commanded the squadron, Philip led 92 away from the Bump at 2.15 p.m., linking up with their sister unit 72 near Hornchurch, before turning steeply and heading south towards Maidstone. Enemy vapour trails were clearly visible to the south-east, and at Angels 20 a large phalanx of German bombers passed below with no sign of accompanying fighters.

Eagerly accepting this blessing, Sanders ordered line-astern, flinging his mount X4051 into a spectacular peel-off to starboard, which brought him directly above and behind his opponents. The twin-engined bombers were Dornier 17Zs of KG2 or 3, which were long and lean with twin fins and rudders, and all too often mistaken for the somewhat similar Messerschmitt 110s in the heat of combat. There was no doubting their identity on this day, however, as Philip concentrated on a target hanging in on the right of the swarm, steadying his Spitfire for a long, five-second burst as he closed to the point-blank range of seventy-five yards. Large fragments were blasted away from the Dornier's

Left: *A photograph of Philip Sanders later in the war, after his operational service had finished.* (P.J. Sanders)
Right: *Twenty-four years after they had last posed together (see top picture on p.55), Sanders and Billy Drake appeared together at a No.1 Squadron reunion in 1962, shortly before the former's retirement as an air commodore.* (P.J. Sanders)

fuselage and starboard engine as his tracer converged on the high-winged raider. As he broke away, he clearly saw one crewman take to his parachute. The Dornier wobbled, behaving 'in an erratic manner', with smoke pouring from its stricken motor as he saw it falling away in a steep dive. He was credited with a Do 17Z destroyed on this day, in a squadron total of nine kills in two actions, on a day when the Luftwaffe threw its whole might against the capital and was soundly repulsed. Sixty German aircraft failed to return from operations, and the enemy high command had to admit that the RAF, far from being finished, was, in fact, gaining strength.

Sanders gained his last kill, an Me 109 on 20 September, while flying X4418, a brand-new machine which had only recently been delivered. Ten aircraft of 92 Squadron scrambled at 11.15 a.m. to rendezvous with 41 Squadron over Gravesend. 41 failed to appear, and Gannic Squadron were ordered to climb to 20,000 feet to intercept a high-altitude raid. The Controller then vectored the Spitfires south, demanding a climb to 27,000 feet in the face of bright sunshine. At around 11.45 a.m., highly vulnerable as they continued to rise in formation over Dungeness, Blue Section were bounced by 109s of JG51, led by the noted German ace, Werner Molders. He shot down and killed PO Howard Hill and Sergeant Peter Eyles, the other Spitfires rapidly scattering as the Messerschmitts flashed through them. Sanders knew the enemy fighters were about and had just broadcast a warning over the R/T when he saw them closing. He broke swiftly to port, glimpsing a 109 also turning left behind him. As it passed below, Philip gave it a quick burst from above and to the right at a distance of 120 yards. The 109 immediately went into the standard evasion tactic, half-rolling to starboard and diving steeply away. Sanders was close behind as his quarry plunged at a sharp angle for some 10,000 feet before levelling out, perhaps unaware that a vengeful Spitfire was hot on his heels. As the German warplane straightened out, he received a withering close-range spraying from the CO's eight Brownings from directly above and behind, and again broke away in a second urgent effort to escape. The Derbyshireman pursued him to the end, firing intermittently and only pulling out of his steepening dive at 500 feet, as his doomed victim went straight into the Channel 5 miles south of Dymchurch. He had expended 2,450 rounds in dispatching his final adversary.

Three days later, Philip Sanders was out of the Battle, not as the result of enemy action, but of the overzealous attentions of his batman. Even this accident has been the subject of misinformation, and the circumstances of the mishap have been romanticised. As recently as 1994, one account still insisted that he landed after an interception patrol with his clothes soaked in petrol as a result of battle damage and lit a cigarette, thereby setting himself on fire. Events prompting his injury were far more prosaic; Philip's uniform jacket had picked up an oil stain, which his batman removed with the aid of 100-octane petrol. On his arrival at dispersal, wearing the newly-cleaned item, he did indeed light up a cigarette and his hands were immediately engulfed in flames. These were rapidly beaten out and the CO was rushed to hospital for treatment. The burns were not serious, but he was *hors de combat* for a month. His replacement lasted a fortnight before he gashed his hands breaking out of his cockpit after a crash. Brian Kingcome took over until the arrival of the Canadian Johnny Kent.

History has been less than just to Sanders and his period of command with 92. A former squadron pilot has commented that, after Bushell, 'we had a succession of almost unnoticed COs ... as a consequence we worked things out for ourselves.' This hardly seems fair or even correct. Sanders served with 92 for almost four months, emerging as a fighter ace with six combat victories and a decoration, which are hardly results attributable to an 'unnoticed' commanding officer. It must have been more than a little comfort to him, as he rested with bandaged hands that October, to learn that he had been awarded the Distinguished Flying Cross. The citation read:

Squadron Leader Sanders has commanded his squadron since May 1940, and his continuous leadership, skill and determination has been responsible for the high standard and morale of the squadron. On 11 September when leading his squadron on an offensive patrol, he displayed great skill and leadership and was personally responsible for the destruction of two, and possibly three hostile aircraft. He has in all destroyed at least six enemy aircraft.

In late October Sanders was posted to Headquarters 11 Group, which was a new job connected with night-fighter operations. He served there for some six months, helping to develop an effective night-fighter organisation. In May 1941, he became CO of 264 Squadron, flying Defiant turret-fighters equipped with pilot-operated AI radar. There were many teething troubles with this apparatus, and in a period of experimentation the unit worked with the ill-starred 'Turbinlite' Havocs, fitted with nose-mounted Helmore searchlights. In December Sanders was promoted to wing commander and was subsequently posted to the United States, where he worked with the USAAF at Wright Field on the development of American fighter aircraft. It was an interesting appointment; he flew a variety of experimental and production fighters, including the first US jet aeroplane, the Bell Airacomet. He was also involved in the development of the P51 Mustang as a long-range escort fighter. Sanders returned to England as Wing Commander Training and Tactics, based with HQ 84 Group, Allied Expeditionary Air Force. In February 1945 he was a group captain commanding an OTU at Petan Tiqua in Palestine, attending the RAF Staff College in Haifa. When in Palestine, he routinely examined the logbooks of South African pilots on a course, and found to his surprise that the Hawker Furies relinquished by his old squadron, No.1, in early 1939 at Tangmere, had found their way to the SAAF and been used against the Italians in Abyssinia!

After the war, Philip reverted to the peacetime rank of wing commander. He was Wg Cdr Air Tactics and Training at the Air Ministry from 1945 to 1947, and then took the Service's Russian language course at the School of Slavonic Studies at London University, before spending three years as air attaché in Belgrade at the time of Tito's quarrel with Stalin. In 1951 he was Wg Cdr Admin at Coltishall – then operating Mosquitoes and later Meteor NF11s.

In January 1952 he was promoted to group captain, and attended a six-month staff course at the Joint Services Staff College. From 1953 to 1955 he commanded the All-Weather Operational Conversion Unit at RAF Leeming, followed by a posting to Paris as Gp Capt. Operations (Air Defence Division) at SHAPE. He then commenced a memorable tour of duty as Air Attaché in Moscow, from 1958 to 1961, at the height of the Kruschev era. He achieved Air rank in 1961 with his promotion to Air Commodore Operations at HQ Fighter Command. This was his final posting, and he retired after a distinguished and varied career in 1962. Regrettably no other honours came his way to mark his long service and commitment as a career officer. His rank was certainly the highest achieved by a Derbyshire fighter pilot post-war, and may well be the highest of any local airman of that era. After his retirement, he worked for fourteen years at the MOD as a civil servant.

The Sanders had three children – two boys and a girl – who between them produced eight grandchildren. After his military service, Philip retired to Northiam in Sussex, where he died in January 1989 at the age of seventy-seven. He remains a man whose contribution to the war effort, especially in 1940, has been obscured by ignorance and omission. Certainly he deserved better of aviation historians, and I can but hope that this account will allow him, albeit posthumously, the credit he deserves. He bore an irksome cross leading the self-proclaimed 'wild and undisciplined ... bolshie bunch of bastards' of 92 into combat. The record shows that as an unproved CO who overcame obstacles to claim six enemy victims and a DFC for his 'continuous leadership, skill and determination', he did not, on reflection, do such a bad job.

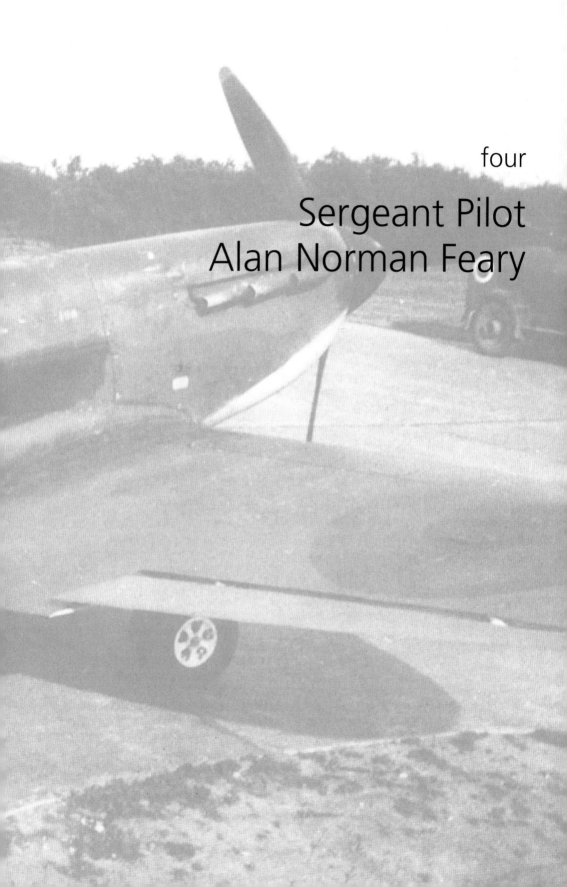

four

Sergeant Pilot
Alan Norman Feary

Combat Record

Date	Sqn	Locality	Aircraft Flown	Enemy Type	Claim
18.07.40	609	S. of Swanage	Spitfire I L1008 PR–K	Junkers 88A	Destroyed (shared)
12.08.40	609	Isle of Wight	Spitfire I N3223 PR–M	Messerschmitt 109E	Destroyed
13.08.40	609	Lyme Bay	Spitfire I L1065 PR–E	Junkers 87B Messerschmitt 110C	Destroyed Damaged
14.08.40	609	Boscombe Down	Spitfire I L1065 PR–E	Junkers 88A	Destroyed
25.08.40	609	Wareham	Spitfire I R6691 PR–J	Messerschmitt 110C Messerschmitt 110C	Destroyed Damaged
07.09.40	609	Broxbourne Redhill	Spitfire I X4234 PR–B	Messerschmitt 109E Junkers 88A	Probable Damaged
24.09.40	609	Isle of Wight	Spitfire I X4234 PR–B	Messerschmitt 110C	Destroyed
25.09.40	609	Bristol	Spitfire I X4234 PR–B	Messerschmitt 110C	Damaged
26.09.40	609	Southampton	Spitfire I X4234 PR–B	Messerschmitt 109E	Damaged

A 1940 studio portrait of Sergeant Pilot Alan Norman Feary. (D. Drake-Feary)

Sergeant Pilot Alan Norman Feary

ALAN NORMAN FEARY was born in Derby in April 1912, to Thomas Feary, a horse inspector employed by the Midland Railway, and Maud Victoria, née Steele. His father died when Alan was only six, and he was brought up by his widowed mother. He had a younger half-brother, Harry Press-Dee Morgan, and a step-brother, Leigh Morgan. Alan was educated at the Derby Municipal Secondary School, which later became Bemrose Grammar, and took a local government post at the borough treasurer's office in the town. Former colleagues remember him as good company, neatly dressed and self-assured. He developed an early interest in cars and motorcycles, and his first vehicle – an Austin Seven with a strapped-down bonnet – cost him all of £5!

He was also remembered as a charmer, whose aquiline looks, broad shoulders and height, plus a polite and self-effacing manner, made him popular with the opposite sex. He dabbled in local amateur dramatics and was an energetic sportsman, excelling in cricket and football, whilst as a tennis player he represented his county in the mixed doubles. His interest in motor vehicles and his proficiency in ball games demanding instant reflexes provided a useful training for his true *metier*, which he discovered after the formation of the RAFVR in July 1936. The RAFVR formed part of a scheme to expand the Service and provide sufficient pilots in time of war. The upper age limit was twenty-five, so Alan was only just eligible for training.

Chosen spare-timers learned to fly at weekends, with fees paid by the RAF, and on gaining their wings received the rank of sergeant. They also attended compulsory evening classes, usually in winter, and studied aircraft armament, the theory of flight, aero-engineering, signals and navigation at the RAFVR centre at Highfields. Comprehensive air training on Tiger Moths, Magisters and Harts took place at Burnaston Aerodrome, between Derby and Burton-on-Trent. It was later to become No.30 Elementary and Reserve Flying Training School, and has now been swept away for the establishment of the Toyota car factory.

Alan found his true vocation as he climbed into the skies over South Derbyshire, growing in competence and skill as he mastered the machines he flew. He received his flying badge and promotion to sergeant pilot on 18 November 1938. Among his contemporaries was Denis Crowley-Milling, then an apprentice at Rolls-Royce, and who later became a distinguished fighter pilot, and after a lifetime career in the RAF achieved Air rank and was duly knighted.

The RAFVR were mobilised on 1 September 1939, following the German invasion of Poland after the cynical Ribbentrop-Molotov pact made war inevitable. Alan was posted to No.9 FTS in December, and advanced from basic trainers to more up-to-date monoplanes with refinements such as retractable undercarriages, hydraulic flaps and variable-pitch airscrews. By April 1940 he had progressed to No.5 OTU at Aston Down, near Stroud, a less-than-pleasant experience for the fledgling aviator as he was drafted on to twin-motor Blenheim 1Fs. These were light bombers, adapted as long-range fighters by the addition of four-gun belly packs under their fuselages. These lumbering warplanes made less-than-successful fighters, being slower than many of the bombers they were supposed to intercept. They also bore an uncomfortably close resemblance to the German Junkers 88A.

On 11 May, one day after Hitler's assault on the West was launched, Alan was posted to 600 Squadron based at Manston, doubtless noting that this unit flew the Blenheim 1F, which was not the sort of aeroplane to appeal to a flier with visions of piloting a Hurricane or Spitfire in combat. Fortunately, fate took a hand at this point. 600 moved to Northolt on the 16th, and two days later were joined by the sleek, racy-looking Spitfires of 609 (West Riding) Squadron, which were moved south from Drem in Scotland. 609 was an Auxiliary Squadron, the RAF equivalent of the Territorials. These units initially consisted of young men from comfortable, not to say affluent, backgrounds. They were recruited to form part-time, locally-based groups attached to certain cities and counties. Absorbed into the RAF at the outbreak of war, one-quarter of our fighter resources in 1940 were from the AAF. Some servicemen derided these peacetime amateur formations as 'rather snobbish preserves of the rich', but their ranks

Alan in flying gear at Burnaston aerodrome in the summer of 1939. Behind him is the now-demolished Burnaston House, HQ of the Flying School. Rather poignantly, this whole area is now covered by the Derby Toyota car factory. (J. Jackson)

Alan, in white overalls, discusses the day's activities with fellow trainees, who include, from left to right: Denis Crowley-Milling, Harold Hunt, and ? Ryan on the right. Crowley-Milling and Hunt became distinguished fliers during the Second World War. Note the Tiger Moth and Magister elementary trainers and the smoke wind-direction marker. (D. Drake-Feary)

Hawker Audax K3707 (on the left) and Hind K5547 trainers line up at Burnaston in the spring of 1939, with the latter warming up ready for take-off. Feary can be seen on the right, just in front of the balding civilian type. (J. Jackson)

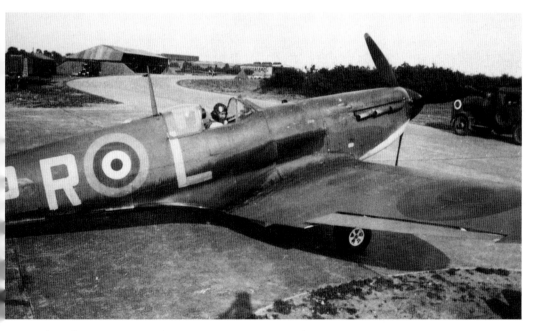

Pilot Officer David Crook of 609 Squadron warms up Spitfire R6699 PR-L at Northolt in June 1940. Note the Albion petrol bowser on the right and the Hurricane on the perimeter track in the distance. Alan joined 609 on the 11th of this month at Northolt. (Squadron Archives)

The jubilant 609 pilots at Warmwell after the action against the Stukas on 13 August. Feary stands third from right, and the CO, Darley, is fifth from right. David Crook is kneeling, centre front. The basic facilities of the forward base are shown to (dis)advantage. (Squadron Archives)

included well-educated young men with high morale and fitness. They also tended to be older than either their opponents or their equivalents in the regular RAF fighter squadrons.

Within a short time, 609 were thrown into the vortex of Dunkirk. In the intensive combats in support of the operations to rescue the BEF, no fewer than five of their number were killed. To 'make good' the losses, pilots were drafted in from the nearest available source – regular, AAF or VR. This produced a leavening effect on the squadron, who shortly added two Poles and three Americans to their ranks. The unit should perhaps have been withdrawn for rest and recuperation, but perhaps due to official recognition of its basic fibre, it was kept in the front line.

Alan Feary, who was one of three pilots posted to the squadron on 11 June, was lucky on two counts. A new squadron commander, H.S. 'George' Darley, had just taken over. Darley was an experienced pilot, who, despite his diminutive size, speedily knocked the unit into shape, shaking the pilots out of their self-pity over the Dunkirk losses and raising their morale and fighting spirit. The second important plus-factor was that 609 flew Spitfire Is, the only fighter capable of tackling the formidable Messerschmitt 109E on even terms. The lethal 109 made mincemeat of all other fighter opposition of the period, outclassing the other RAF interceptor, the Hurricane, on all counts except manoeuvrability. Therefore, the Derbyshire pilot flew the best his country could supply, aircraft powered by Rolls-Royce Merlin engines built in his native town.

On 15 June, Alan had 50 minutes of instruction in Harvard P5865 under the expert eye of Flight-Commander Frank Howell, to familiarise himself with the advanced features of modern low-wing monoplanes; he was then thought capable of transferring to the Spitfire. In early July, with Darley doing his utmost to train his new pilots to a level where they might reasonably expect to survive, 609 was moved to a newly-built base at Middle Wallop, south-west of Andover. They also used the rather uninviting Sector airfield at Warmwell near Dorchester as a forward base, patrolling over coastal convoys and the important Portland-Southampton area. Early operations showed that tactics and ground control were sadly deficient, and 609 were all too often sent out against superior forces in penny-packet numbers. As a result three pilots, including two flight-commanders, were lost in two patrols on 9 July, and the outlook for the survivors appeared bleak indeed.

Feary's own baptism took place on 18 July and taught a salutary lesson. Red Section, 'A' Flight, led by Flt Lt Howell with FO Edge as Red 2 and Alan as Red 3, were vectored onto a lone Junkers 88 of either 1/KG54 or II/LG1 in cloudy weather off the Dorset coast. The three Spitfires picked up the raider which immediately dived away seawards, jettisoning its bombs. The fighters attacked in turns, with Feary in L1008 (PR-K) being the last to open fire. Both his companions were hit by return fire from the enemy rear-gunner – a fine piece of shooting, considering the single low-calibre MG15 machine gun carried by the Ju 88A for rearward defence. Edge had to crash-land on Studland Beach, where his aircraft was later engulfed by the rising tide, while Howell baled out over the sea and was rescued by launch. After Feary's second attack, the raider was down to sea level, with both engines on fire. It duly crashed into the Channel off Hengistbury Head, but Alan was the only pilot from Red Section to return bearing the news of a rather chastening clash!

During July, 609 flew more sorties – generally convoy patrols – than any other squadron in Fighter Command. Throughout this period, as well as teaching his new pilots the tricks of the trade, Darley experimented with new battle formations, and was aware of the limitations of the standard RAF vic of three when opposed by Me 109s, who worked in pairs and fours, which were far more flexible tactical units than the rigid trios flown by most British fighter squadrons. Eventually Darley operated his command in sections of three in line-astern, which was at least an improvement on the outmoded configurations they had previously used.

The fliers found Middle Wallop a fairly comfortable base, but Warmwell was much more primitive, with poor facilities, tented accommodation, and the infuriating rigidity of mind of the singularly obtuse Station Commander, Wg Cdr George Howard DFC, who refused to allow the pilots proper meals if they failed to appear at the official times! 'All efforts to get the Luftwaffe to respect meal times having failed, a deadlock occurred' is the wry phrase in the squadron diary. The noted fighter pilot Roland Beamont agreed with 609 on the reputation of Warmwell, writing of 'the disorganisation and lack of co-operation which seemed characteristic of that station at that period'.

Sergeant Feary scored his first unaided kill on 12 August, when the enemy launched a heavy attack on the Portsmouth area just after midday. It included 'the whole German Air Force bar Goering', as one wag put it. 609 became entangled with escorting Messerschmitt 110 two-seaters and 109s over the Needles. Alan, flying N3223 PR-M in the Yellow 3 slot, broke through a milling shoal of twin-engined 110s and found a trio of Me 109s circling in front of him. A three-second burst at the rearmost produced no result, but he fastened onto the 109 leader as the enemy pilot dived away to attack two Spitfires below him. Following his opponent into the dive, he thumbed off around ten seconds' worth of .303 ammunition from his eight wing-guns as the German crossed his sights. The enemy fighter flicked over on its back and fell away into a vertical death-dive, plunging towards the sea. He then fought a brisk running battle with the remaining two Messerschmitts until his ammunition was exhausted, and in his own words he 'pushed the red button and came home'. A claim of one Me 109 confirmed was allowed in the first of a series of combat clashes he was involved in over the next few days.

On the 13th, the German *Adlertag* (Eagle Day), 609 were scrambled from Warmwell at 3.30 p.m., with Feary (Red 2) piloting L1065 PR-E. Climbing hard into the sun, the squadron broke

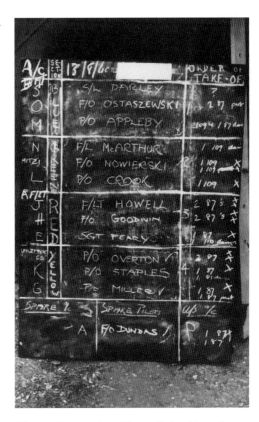

The squadron scoreboard for the lucky thirteenth clearly shows that nearly every pilot claimed for something on that memorable day, when the unit (literally!) chalked up thirteen kills. (Squadron Archives)

through cloud over Lyme Bay, and saw three large vics of Junkers 87B dive bombers of II/StG2 below them, silhouetted against the clouds as they headed for Warmwell. Red Section led the diving attack on the fifty or so inverted gull-winged *Stukas,* lining up on targets in the rear vic. Closing in on his own unsuspecting victim, Feary fired a long twelve-second burst from 250 yards to below a hundred, his tracer riddling the ungainly two-seater with its fixed, spatted undercarriage. His burning quarry fell away, shedding flames and fragments, to plummet into the wide bay below. Climbing at full boost after his attack, he sighted a group of Me 110s below him and dived on the rearmost machine, thumbing a brief burst before turning away. A swift glance behind showed another 110 attempting to get on his tail, but Feary tightened his turn and saw the tracer from his opponent's formidable front armament passing astern. Easily outmanoeuvring the heavy two-seater, the Derbyshire pilot pulled behind his adversary, lining up the Messerschmitt's 53 foot wingspan in his GM2 reflector, and firing his remaining ammunition into it, before breaking away into cloud and heading home. With one victim confirmed and a second damaged, Feary's claims brought 609's score for the action to thirteen, which on subsequent analysis is an exaggeration, but a total which rejuvenated the whole squadron. Their confidence was boosted, and they began to believe in themselves and their own ability.

Alan's third victim was well-authenticated in every way. One witness was PO David Crook, who served in 609 at the time, and mentioned the Derbyshire flier several times in his fine book, *Spitfire Pilot.* At around 5 p.m. on the 14th, Feary (Yellow 2 to the famous FO John Dundas) was piloting PR-E on base patrol over Wallop above an unbroken layer of heavy cloud. Suddenly a Junkers 88 flashed overhead, rapidly seeking cover as Dundas hurtled after it. Feary followed through the thick grey murk, emerging over the airfield in time to see a second 88, of 1/LG1, release a salvo of bombs which straddled the hangars, killing three brave airmen who were attempting to close the massive steel doors of Hangar 5 to protect the Spitfires inside. Retribution was close behind as Alan converged on the diving Junkers over Boscombe Down, squeezing his firing button at 250 yards and seeing most of the 2,800 rounds from his eight Brownings slam into the bandit. Feary pulled away as the raider's dive steepened; it crashed and exploded on the down-land, around 5 miles from the airfield. Many of 609's pilots were at readiness in their cockpits and, following the sudden attack, took off in a wild scramble. Crook himself was swiftly airborne, turning south-west to over-fly the blazing funeral pyre of the unfortunate German. He later reported he 'had never seen an aeroplane so thoroughly wrecked; it was an awful mess.' Feary was duly presented with the rubber dinghy from the shot-down bomber as a trophy. He later sent it to the Mayor of Derby's War Fund and it was duly placed on exhibition in the town.

Alan landed at Wallop at 5.25 p.m., but took off again after refuelling and re-arming. He climbed to 11,000 feet, aiming to get above the cloud base. He quickly picked out four Ju 88s in diamond formation, heading south-west at 16,000 feet, and climbed above them as they swung eastward. The four bandits then headed north-west, and finally south, as Feary decided to launch a lone attack on the starboard warplane. A four-second burst produced no result, nor did two further doses aimed at two other bombers in the formation. Feary reported no return fire and broke away with his ammunition exhausted. He was only airborne for twenty minutes and landed at 6 p.m. for further replenishment. As odd enemy bombers were still putting in an appearance, Alan took off for a third time, circling the base below cloud level. Almost immediately, another Ju 88 approached Wallop and released a string of bombs. Feary slammed open his throttle and closed with his assailant, who rapidly sought and found cloud cover. The Derbyshire pilot followed the bomber into the murk and fired off short intermittent bursts, as pursuer and pursued emerged briefly through gaps in the cloud. The Junkers eventually disappeared, and a disappointed Alan came home when instructed by 'Bandy' Control. He had experienced a busy late afternoon, firing on no less than five raiders, but could only claim the one very definitely confirmed.

As the August days progressed, Alan remained in a somewhat unique position in the squadron, as he was the only sergeant pilot within the unit. One later writer thought 'he must have felt dreadfully lonely', although his CO believed he had a number of friends among the NCO pilots of the other squadrons based at Wallop. However, another 609 pilot, PO John 'Bishop' Bisdee, did think Alan was a lone figure

Feary had several early clashes with the formidable Junkers 88A, like the one photographed here, shooting down two, and damaging a third in three separate combats.

The shattered wreckage of the 1/LG1 bomber shot down by Feary on 14 August lies strewn across Boscombe Down, with avid juvenile souvenir hunters sifting for mementoes. An airman from the base poses behind a battered-looking wing. (Squadron Archives)

Four views showing the destruction wrought by Alan's victim on Hangar 5 at Wallop. In this shot the flattened thirteen-ton hangar doors lie on the right. Between them and the pitted wall there is a 604 Squadron Blenheim I. Three airmen were crushed underneath the doors as they desperately tried to close them to protect the aircraft inside. (S.H. Hanson)

Another shot of the devastated hangar, which was literally blown apart by the explosion of the Junkers' bombs. (S.H. Hanson)

Three Spitfires of 609 Squadron were smashed beyond repair by the enemy bombs. The cameraman looks towards the doors, alongside the engine cowling of one machine. The graceful wing of another Spitfire leans drunkenly in the middle distance. (S.H. Hanson)

The view from Hangar 4 shows the same Spitfire wing just inside the hangar on the right, as well as the flattened doors, and gives a good idea of the great size of the structure. Note how the bombs have blasted the hangar roof to matchwood. Hangar 5 remained in ruins for a number of years after its blitzing. (S.H. Hanson)

The Middle Wallop dispersal in August 1940. The tall figure of Alan can be seen on the right; David Crook is the central pilot wearing a Mae West and holding a mug of tea; the CO, Darley, likewise attired, is on Crook's right. Tin-hatted ground crew complete the ensemble. (Squadron Archives)

Spitfire R6769 PR-D at rest. Its condition is courtesy of FO Dundas who attempted to land on a Bofors gun position during night practice. The remains of Hangar 5 can be seen on the right. Alan Feary flew this aircraft operationally on several occasions; note the three kill emblems below the cockpit. (M.J.F. Bowyer)

in the sense that he had little contact with his higher-ranking colleagues once off-duty. Alan was a victim of the ridiculous barrier between NCO and officer pilots, who flew the same aircraft and faced the same dangers, but who were rigidly segregated on the ground. The idea that the whole system was a nonsense is shown by the large numbers of NCO aircrew who later gained commissions, high rank and decorations as the war progressed.

Alan Feary next fired his guns in anger on 25 August. In the late afternoon of that day, an enemy raid of over a hundred approached Warmwell, which consisted of 45 Junkers 88s protected by Me 109s and 110s. 609 were rapidly scrambled to protect their forward base, with Darley shrewdly leading his Spitfires high above the German fighter cover before bringing them down in line-astern to fall upon the 110 escort. Alan took off as Red 4 – the usual spare pilot position – in R6691 PR-J, the usual mount of Frank Howell, but switched to Yellow 3 before the attack commenced. With fourteen Spitfires swooping among them like predatory birds, the lumbering 110s of ZG2 broke in all directions. Feary put a burst, at 150 yards, into the long cockpit greenhouse of his target, seeing his tracer strike home before the *Zerstörer* curved away beneath him. Claiming precious height, he snapped off short bursts at a formation of two-seaters ahead and out to sea. Leaving them to it, he turned PR-J back towards the coast, crossing Lulworth Cove at 15,000 feet. Over Coombe Keynes he picked out a lone 110 below him, heading north. He slipped his Spitfire behind his unseeing adversary, hammering out a long ten-second burst as he framed the twin-finned escort in the glowing circle of his gunsight. White smoke gushed from the port motor, and the wounded crew lost no time in baling out of their stricken warplane, which nosed over into a vertical dive, engines snarling, and smashed into the ground at Creech Barrow at 5.45 p.m. The enemy pilot was Oblt Goetz, Staffelführer of 1/ZG2, his gunner Uffz. Haupt. The 110, coded 3M+AH, was one of seven claimed in the teatime mêlée, with no corresponding loss. A few pieces of the impacted wreckage of Alan's Messerschmitt were recovered during site excavations in the 1970s.

At the beginning of September, 609 Squadron were an experienced and highly efficient unit, seasoned with a cadre of veteran pilots, who were combat-honed and boasted a high morale. They were switched to factory protection patrols encompassing the West London area on the Northolt-Brooklands-Windsor line. The Spitfires were operating at maximum range, having as far to fly to their London patrol line as an Me 109 based behind Calais. On 7 September the Luftwaffe launched its first heavy daylight raids on the capital, and in the late afternoon 609 were directed to support 11 Group by pursuing withdrawing enemy formations flying over the city. Bursting anti-aircraft fire showed the pilots where the enemy were – over 200 of them, heading back home. Alan was piloting X4234 PR-B, a Spitfire he flew throughout the month and which was presumably his personal machine. Flying in the Yellow 2 position, he sparred briefly with a shoal of 110s, before climbing to 14,000 feet north of the city, where he picked out a pair of Me 109s who were flying along steadily and foolishly maintaining a straight and level course. The enemy fliers seemed comparative tyros, as they failed to spot the sergeant pilot approaching from above and behind. Choosing the wingman, Alan raked his slender, square-winged target with a four-second burst, closing from 250 yards to less than a hundred. His victim fell away dragging a stream of black smoke, but he could not watch its end as the second 109 turned to attack. Feary broke away and lost his opponent. Alan's attack took place at around 5.30 p.m. and two Me 109s of JG51 crashed in Kent shortly after this time, with both pilots baling out of their stricken fighters. One of these kills may well have been his. PR-B climbed hard over the Thames, its pilot watching shell-bursts clustering thickly around another enemy gaggle. Over Redhill he intercepted a flock of Ju 88s heading south, and launched a beam attack on a lone straggler. A long burst from his eight Brownings, commencing at 450 yards and closing to point-blank range, raked the bomber, silencing the rear gunner and punching ragged holes in the Junkers' tail unit. Almost out of ammunition, and with other enemy aircraft closing on him from astern, Alan called it a day, diving steeply and landing at Tangmere to refuel before heading home. He claimed an Me 109 probable and a Ju 88 damaged in this lively late-afternoon engagement.

After a spell of leave, during which he missed the mass German assault on London on 15 September, which later became Battle of Britain day, Alan returned to continue the fight. By this time he was obviously a well-regarded and thoroughly reliable professional – one of 609's stalwarts. His Spitfire had never been hit by enemy fire, and he had avoided the niggling and annoying accidental damage caused to some of the squadron's aircraft by carelessness or bad luck, all details of which were meticulously recorded in *Ye Booke,* the unofficial squadron diary written by Flight Sergeant 'Tich' Cloves, ground staff NCO in charge of 'A' Flight.

His first combat after the London battle took place on the 24th. Bad weather had hampered Luftwaffe operations after the 15th, but on the day in question they returned to the south-west, launching an attack on the Supermarine works at Woolston near Southampton. 609 Squadron intercepted the raid at 4.20 p.m., by Messerschmitt 110 bombers of the crack ErpG 210, escorted by Me 110s of ZG76 and 109s, north of the Isle of Wight. The squadron clashed with a mass of aircraft identified as Dornier 17s. These were without doubt bomb-carrying 110s; both types were often misidentified during the Battle as from certain angles they looked disturbingly alike. Piloting PR-B in the Red 2 position, Alan squeezed off several bursts at a group of 'Dorniers' hanging together in a broad vic, before a quick warning in his earphones forced him to break away as yellow-nosed Me 109s bore down on the squadron out of the sun. Alan gained height as the 109s rapidly disappeared, and picked up the departing 110s as they crossed the Isle of Wight. He noticed one laggard dragging behind the rest, exhausts vomiting smoke trails as the pilot opened his throttles in a vain effort to keep up with his comrades. The Derbyshire pilot steadily closed the gap; from dead astern, he pumped in a four-second burst. The Messerschmitt hauled round to port with X4234 hanging doggedly behind it, raking it for a further five seconds before the German's nose fell away in a steepening dive. The 110, losing first its wings and then its tail unit, finally crashed into the Channel thousands of feet below, off Brightstone Bay.

David Crook provided a graphic account of the action. From some half-mile astern, he witnessed Feary's attack and saw his victim turn over on its back and go into a spin. 'It was rather a shaking sight', he wrote:

> *Down he went, spinning faster and faster at an incredible rate for such a big machine, and then suddenly a wing was wrenched off. The Dornier [sic] gave a lurch and continued to dive, but now crazily turning over and over ... I saw the other wing and the tail break away, and the fuselage then went straight down like a stone and disappeared from sight. A moment later, looking down, I saw a patch of foam appear on the sea over 20,000 feet below, showing where he had dropped.*

This well-authenticated kill brought Alan's official score to five and one shared, and was his last confirmed claim.

Alan fired his guns in two more combats, but was only able to claim damage to two further enemy aircraft. Late on the morning of 25 September, 609 tangled with Me 110 escorts of ZG26 screening Heinkel IIIs of KG55 attacking the Bristol Aeroplane Company's works at Filton, north of the city. The squadron again identified the 110s as Dorniers, with Darley leading an interception down-sun against three large arrowhead formations of Messerschmitts. Flying X4234, Alan was leading Yellow Section, following Red into action. He pumped tracer into a mass of tightly-packed raiders before breaking away and climbing. More Me 110s were above. From below he launched a beam attack on one, thumbing a two-second burst at 300 yards and seeing coolant vapour stream from his target's port engine as he broke and climbed again. He met a gaggle of 110s climbing up behind the main formation and latched on behind, delivering a three-second burst at 300 yards and seeing black smoke spew from his latest victim's port motor. Another 110 appeared in front, but two short bursts emptied his magazines, and, his thirsty Merlin having consumed over 80 gallons of 100-octane, he landed at Yeovil to refuel and re-arm.

Opposite above: A fine shot of the squadron ground crew posing by Spitfire PR-H at a muddy Warmwell in the autumn of 1940. PR-G is in the background, with the trolley acc. plugged in. The photograph picks out the salient features of the MkI Spitfires to perfection, including the doped patches covering the eight wing guns. (Squadron Archives)

Left: *Alan's tombstone in the churchyard of Holy Trinity, Warmwell, pays tribute to his status as 'One of the Few'. Other Battle of Britain pilots are interred in the same plot.* (Author) Above: *Alan was not the only member of his family to die in the Second World War. His half-brother, Harry Press-Dee Morgan, was killed in August 1941, flying Spitfires with 41 Squadron.* (F. Claydon)

'Four-second burst at 200 yards.' Alan Feary dictates his combat report to Pilot Officer Mackay, the 609 Squadron Intelligence Officer. (Squadron Archives)

The following day at around 4 p.m. the unit were once more in action. 59 Heinkel IIIs of KG55, again protected by 109s and 110s, flying on a five-mile front up the Solent, went for the Supermarine Aviation Works on the waterfront at Woolston, releasing 70 tons of high explosive in a single pass over the factory. 609, sent off too late and too low, were unable to stop the Heinkels hitting the target so hard that Spitfire production was halted for a time. Darley ordered 'A' Flight to take on the fighters and 'B' Flight, to take on the bombers. Alan, Yellow 3, again in X4234, yelled a warning as four yellow-nosed 109s approached his Section from the east, and the Spitfires broke away in all directions. Feary went on alone to engage a swarm of Heinkels passing below, which was the first time he had met these adversaries in the air. Boring in from abeam, he squeezed the firing-button at 400 yards, closing rapidly to 200, but saw no strikes. No wonder, considering the fast-moving pass against a mass target. As he dived away he was attacked from astern by a single 109, feeling bullet strikes hitting his Spitfire. Fortunately the German pilot overshot his target and ended up in that most dangerous position, in front of his intended quarry. As the Messerschmitt pulled round in a fast climbing turn, Feary held it in his sights for four seconds, seeing his fire disappear into its engine and the underside of its pale blue fuselage, before he lost it. Seeking further targets, he saw the enemy bombers streaming back out to sea, but they were too far away to be caught. He noted a parachute lazily descending, and was ordered by 'Bandy' Control to remain on patrol until his petrol was low. He then turned PR-B back to base to make his final combat claim – one Messerschmitt 109E damaged. The composite Fighter Command combat report stated that his Spitfire returned with a damaged spar, and Flight Sergeant Cloves' squadron diary did record bullet holes in his machine, which was the first time his aeroplane had been hit in combat. Cloves also recorded that whilst landing the squadron Magister N3239 at Weston Zoyland the following day, Alan hit a large screw picket, injuring the starboard main-plane and flaps.

Sadly the tenacious Derbyshire flier did not survive the Battle. On 4 October Sqn Ldr Darley was posted and replaced by Michael Robinson, who proved equally as competent a leader, though in a different way. On the 7th Robinson led his new squadron for the first time. The afternoon was glaringly bright and visibility was exceptional. It was the sort of day when high-flying 109s could bounce unsuspecting opponents with ease in the dazzle. At 20,000 feet, a cluster of Ju 88s was seen over Weymouth, returning from a raid on the Westland Aircraft Factory at Yeovil. Protecting them were a number of screening Me 110s, and sections of yellow-nosed 109s in line-astern above. 'A' Flight, with Alan in the veteran N3238, opened formation as they saw the 109s. Robinson ordered sections line-astern and the Spitfires went into action against a circle of 110s ahead. Alan, concentrating on the targets ahead of him, was probably hit by a 109 of JG2 coming from above and behind in the glare. He broke away, but the enemy's fire must have damaged his controls and his Spitfire fell away in a spin. Struggling hard, he pulled out after losing precious height, but N3238 immediately flicked into a second deadly gyration. He righted his fighter a second time, only for the impaired controls to cause a third fatal oscillation almost immediately. Desperate to level his aeroplane, he only appreciated his personal danger too late. He should have baled out immediately when his Spitfire was hit – aircraft were far more expendable than the pilots who flew them. When he finally ejected, he had left it too late. He cleared his doomed fighter easily, but his parachute had no time to deploy, and his body, partly covered by his half-open canopy, was found at Watercombe Farm, which was less than a mile from the airfield at Warmwell which he was doubtless hopelessly trying to reach.

N3238 crashed and burned out not far away. The squadron diary perhaps encapsulated Alan's attitude and attachment to the machines he flew, and some prescient hand, possibly that of John Dundas, wrote of him:

He seemed to regard his Spitfire with the kind of jealous care and affection that some others bestow upon animals, and the notion has been advanced by those who knew him well that this trait in his character

In May 1987 the author, left, handed over Alan Feary's medals and other memorabilia to Brian Waters, the curator of Derby Industrial Museum. They were for incorporation in the permanent display to the fighter pilot's memory, which was officially opened on 2 July. Here, the exhibits rest on a Merlin engine of 1940 vintage. (Derby Evening Telegraph)

may have contributed to the loss of his life, causing reluctance to bale out from a spin which he was unable to control.

It may well be true that Alan's love for his aircraft was the one real love of his life, and there is no doubting his feelings for the three tons of streamlined metal that bore him into battle.

Buried with full military honours in the small churchyard at Holy Trinity, Warmwell, Alan lies in a scrupulously maintained War Grave cemetery. Tributes by his squadron companions were generous and sincere. David Crook called him 'a very good and resolute pilot' and the squadron diary 'a very good pilot ... steady and painstaking'. Thirty years later Darley was to describe him as 'most reliable at all times. I never found a single fault in him.' Few men could wish a better epitaph. Darley also remembered Alan as 'worthy and reliable, and a very sad loss to 609.' Michael Robinson had the unenviable task of writing to his mother about the fellow airman he hardly knew. 'His reputation as a brave and fearless fighter pilot was handed over to me by his previous commanding officer', he wrote in his letter of sympathy, 'and I can say that he died as he would have wished – for his country. It would be difficult to tell you how much he will be missed by his fellow pilots.' A further tribute came at the meeting of the Derby Town Council on 8 October, when Alderman C.R. Bates remarked 'we all appreciate what he did, and we are proud of him.'

Frank Ziegler, who chronicled the history of 609 Squadron in the Second World War, wrote of Alan Feary's 'distinction that should have earned him a decoration'. It must remain a blot on someone's escutcheon that he failed to gain an award, especially since five of his flying comrades received Distinguished Flying Crosses that autumn, and two of them had combat records very similar to that of Alan. With five confirmed kills, plus one shared, one probable and no less than five enemy aircraft damaged, he was at least as worthy as any of his fellow flyers. Regrettably he received neither honours nor acknowledgement in life or in death: a sad and sorry omission by his superiors. Certainly, many fighter pilots were decorated for fewer victories. It is a matter of record that, throughout the war, only four sergeant pilots won bravery awards whilst serving with 609, as against forty officers, which, if it proves anything, shows that the squadron was not overgenerous to its NCO pilots. Was Alan Feary the forgotten ace?

It is fitting that Alan's memory was honoured by his native Derby in July 1987. It was an honour I was proud to propose to the city's Industrial Museum, and which was welcomed by many, including his son, David, who was born some six months after his father's death and who is now living at Horsham, Victoria, Australia. It might be appropriate to note that Alan's mother sacrificed two sons during the Second World War. Alan's half-brother, Harry Press-Dee Morgan, joined the RAF in 1941 at the age of nineteen and was killed in action flying Spitfires, like his brother, in August of that year. The memorial in Derby Industrial Museum is an apt tribute to Alan Feary's achievement as one of Derbyshire's twentieth-century sons and warriors whose Spitfire fittingly flew into battle powered by one of the Merlin engines designed and built by the city's most famous engineering firm. We should remember that he was, like others whose careers are chronicled in this work, a volunteer and front-rank representative of the new breed of young, 400 mile-an-hour fighting men, whose gallantry and self-sacrifice saved England, and ultimately the world, from the new Dark Age which would surely have followed a Nazi victory in 1940.

five

Squadron Leader
John Layton Flinders

Combat Record

Date	Sqn	Locality	Aircraft Flown	Enemy Type	Claim
20.11.39	74	Off Southend	Spitfire I K9870	Dornier 17F	Destroyed (shared)
18.05.40	32	Douai	Hurricane I N2463	Heinkel III	Damaged
19.05.40	32	Forêt de Normal	Hurricane I N2463	Messerschmitt 109E	Destroyed
08.06.40	32	Le Treport	Hurricane I N2463	Heinkel III	Destroyed
15.08.40	32	Frant	Hurricane I L2062	Messerschmitt 109E	Destroyed
18.08.40	32	Godstone Harbledown	Hurricane I L2062	Messerschmitt 110C Messerschmitt 110C	Destroyed Destroyed

John as a sergeant pilot with 74 Squadron, is standing in front of one of the unit's Gauntlet fighters in 1938. (J. Flinders)

Squadron Leader John Layton Flinders

JOHN FLINDERS, the lifelong victim to the inevitable, if unoriginal, soubriquet 'Polly' was, like Philip Sanders, a native of Chesterfield. Like Sanders he joined the RAF as a pilot before the war, with the long-term objective of becoming a civilian aviator with Imperial Airways. John was born in August 1917, to Llewellyn, a stonemason, and Nellie Flinders. The family was completed by a younger brother, Peter, who still lives in the town of his birth.

John was educated at Chesterfield Grammar School, which was just a trolleybus ride away from his home at Old Whittington. After matriculation in 1935 he enlisted in the RAF, intending to use this as a stepping-stone into civil aviation. He was accepted as a pilot under training, signing on for four years' active service, followed by six in the reserve, and commencing his *ab initio* instruction at the Bristol Flying School in Filton at the beginning of 1936. His advanced training followed at No.3 Flying Training School in Grantham, on a course lasting from the end of March to December. He was then posted to the famous 74 Tiger Squadron, Hornchurch, as a sergeant pilot.

John loved the Hawker Furies he flew at Grantham, and was exhilarated by the smell of hot oil, the crackling of the open exhausts of the Kestrel in-line engine, and the rush of air around the open cockpit. 74 flew the Gloster Gauntlet, which, with its air-cooled Bristol Mercury radial, did not particularly inspire him, despite the Gauntlet being faster in level flight than the Fury. However, he gained a wealth of experience and a comprehensive grounding in all aspects of Service flying over the next three years with this unit. In 1938 John signed a contract with Imperial Airways at Croydon as a future pilot, and in March 1939 gained the prestigious Air Ministry Navigator's Certificate, which was sadly cancelled on the outbreak of hostilities.

John recalled that pre-war Air Force life was fairly quiet except for rehearsing the mass flights organised to celebrate Empire Air Day and the annual Hendon Air Pageant. On these occasions, 74's Gauntlets would give displays of formation aerobatics, with each aircraft tethered to its neighbour with ribbons. These spectacular manoeuvres were often led by the OC 'A' Flight, the South African Adolph 'Sailor' Malan, who was later a famous ace, and whose signature appears in John's logbook.

In February 1939, 74 became the fourth squadron to re-equip with the Supermarine Spitfire Mk I, a sensational replacement for their ageing open-cockpit biplanes. 'Polly' remembered travelling to Supermarine Aviation's hangars at Eastleigh aerodrome by train, ferrying the new 'wonder planes' with their fixed-pitch, two-blade airscrews back to Hornchurch. To him, going from Gauntlet to Spitfire was like exchanging a Morris Minor for a Ferrari, or a shire horse for a Derby winner.

'It was a delicate, very responsive aeroplane to fly', he wrote in one of his many letters to me, 'with, for those days, fantastic power, speed, and climbing ability.' The only danger was in trying to waffle it down to a landing from twenty feet up, which was standard practice with the Gauntlet. Bent undercarriages were often the result, though John assured me he was never culpable in this respect! His first Spitfire flight was in K9860 on a 40-minute familiarisation, and he and the rest of the pilots soon became operational on their slim, streamlined eight-gun interceptors. In July, 74 Squadron were chosen by the Air Ministry to represent the RAF on the Quatorze Juillet celebrations of the Armée de l'Air at Le Bourget in Paris. They flew out as a full squadron on the 10th, setting a new air speed record – London to Paris in fifty-five minutes. Polly found the sojourn in the French capital to be one long round of receptions and parties. On departure, after a farewell drinks session, all the Spitfires were ballasted with vintage champagne – even the gun ports were loaded with bottles – and the pixilated fliers performed slow-rolls all the way home to Hornchurch. Not one precious bottle was broken, but the return journey took somewhat longer than the outward trip!

When the anticipated war was declared, John was still a sergeant with the unit, and was engaged in the unfortunate Battle of Barking Creek on 6 September. In this ill-fated clash, Sector Control vectored Hurricanes from North Weald and Spitfires from Hornchurch towards each other, believing, for some reason never fully explained, that each was intercepting hostiles. The fighters met west of Ipswich, and

Pilot Officer John Layton Flinders in 1940.
(J. Flinders)

Yellow Section of 74 Squadron opened up on the Hurricanes of 56, shooting down two of them who had taken off without permission, and who were below and behind the rest of their squadron formation. John, Yellow 3, was the only member of his trio not to open fire, though his gunsight was lit and his eight Brownings were armed. Both units broke away, manoeuvring frantically after the initial clash, which resulted in the death of one of 56's fliers. The Sector Controller was duly court-martialled, but no really satisfactory answers were given as to why the appalling mishap occurred.

Action against the real foe did not happen for almost three months. On 20 November 1939, Polly had his first crack at the Luftwaffe, piloting K9870 as Yellow 3 in an interception off Southend in company with FO W.E. Measures and PO R. Temple-Harris. The three Spitfires were prowling around 15 miles east of the seaside town at 20,000 feet, with Measures cruising some way ahead of his companions, as they searched for a lone bandit reported in the vicinity. At 12.45 p.m. they sighted a single contrail above and ahead, etched sharply in white against the deep blue of the sky. The section leader ordered line-astern, and the trio rose to meet the raider, which they identified as a Heinkel III, duly recorded in John's logbook. It was, in fact, a Dornier 17F-1, coded T5+LH, of 1(F)ObdL, engaged on a photographic reconnaissance sortie over London and the Thames Estuary. John was amazed when told that his target of so many years ago was a Dornier, though he admitted that recognition of German aircraft was then an art in its infancy, and 'all we saw and cared about was that the bloody thing had black crosses.'

Spotting the pursuing fighters, the 'Flying Pencil' went into a climb, rising to the considerable height of 27,000 feet before the Spitfires were in a position to fire. Measures attacked first, opening with a two-second burst at 350 yards, as the dark-camouflaged hostile, sporting a white-edged Maltese cross on its fuselage, dived away at high speed, the dorsal gunner returning fire. The section leader had to slam his throttle wide open to keep up, thumbing several short bursts at between 300 and 400 yards, and seeing an object break away from the Dornier as he closed. Suddenly Yellow 1 hit the bandit's slipstream and had to break away to regain control. On landing, Measures realised he had burst his eardrums during the steep 400mph dive.

Temple-Harris and Flinders had kept in contact with their target, and Yellow 2 had followed the Dornier into a cloud layer, firing until the German aircraft disappeared. John saw it break out of the cloud-mass moments later, getting it into his sights and spraying it with his eight Brownings, before his alien high-winged opponent slid away again into concealment. He thus became the first Derbyshire fighter pilot to engage the Luftwaffe in the Second World War, beating Darky Clowes by three days. The badly-damaged Dornier had to ditch off the Essex coast, and the three crewmen were rescued from their dinghy the following day. Polly had opened his account with a third-share of a Dornier definitely destroyed; it was an occasion for congratulation, as the raider was the Tiger Squadron's first kill of the Second World War.

John remained with 74 until April 1940, when he was deservedly commissioned and posted to 32 Squadron at Biggin Hill. The '32nd Pursuit' flew Hurricanes and were soon to be under the command of Sqn Ldr John 'Baron' Worrall. Flinders was not very enthusiastic at his change of mount, exchanging, as he put it, his Ferrari for a family saloon. 'Both aircraft were a delight to fly', he wrote, 'the Spitfire [was] a delicate thoroughbred, highly responsive and challenging you to produce your best. The Hurricane was solid, handling was less responsive, less demanding of your flying skills.' Nevertheless, he was soon to appreciate the virtues of the thick-winged, rugged, hump-backed interceptor flown by his new unit. 32 boasted some skilful fliers, many of whom became well-known aces. They included the tall and slim Mike Crossley, who was given the appellation the 'Red Knight', bestowed in recognition of his leadership of Red Section, 'A' Flight, and apparently because of the talisman chess-piece he fixed on his gunsight. There were also Pete Brothers, 'Grubby' Grice, 'Shag' Exford, 'Humph' Russell, and others. John joined Crossley's section, and was soon at ease in the entertaining and light-hearted company of his new colleagues. When the German *Blitzkrieg* opened on 10 May he went swiftly into action with them.

On 14 May, John took part in a patrol off the Hook of Holland in N2459. At 15,000 feet over the Dutch coast, the pilots saw a huge pall of smoke in the distance. It was only later that they realised it came from the city of Rotterdam, ablaze after a savage German mass bombing earlier in the day. This was 32's first indication of the kind of foe they were facing.

John's first combat with the 32nd Pursuit came four days later. The previous day the unit had been patrolling Northern France, using Abbeville and Dieppe as refuelling stops. On 18 May, he flew in N4260 as part of an escort to Blenheims bombing Arras. He picked out two Heinkel IIIs of 11/KG1, just below cloud near Douai, from which he broke away to attack from behind and abeam in the approved manner. He closed on the nearest, alien in its dark-green splinter camouflage, with its distinctive shape and tall elliptical fin silhouetted in his reflector as he fired. Polly appreciated the good frontal view enjoyed by Hurricane pilots, courtesy of the downward-curving engine cowling, and the steadiness of the machine as a gun-platform. The eight wing-guns, in two close batteries of four, also gave a better concentration of fire than the wider-spaced Brownings along the leading edges of the Spitfire's wing. He squeezed the firing button and saw his tracers converging and sparkling along the Heinkel's fuselage, casually noting return fire which he took to be emanating from a beam gun. Suddenly the windscreen in front of him starred and went partly opaque. It took a second or two for Flinders to realise that a machine gun bullet had hit the armoured glass head-on. As he pulled away, the Heinkel was on its way down, trailing smoke, but his lack of forward vision prevented a follow-up attack. Back at the Bump it was of some consolation to his fellow pilots to realise how effective this frontal protection was. The fitting was removed and put on display in several national exhibitions of war material.

The following day, John was piloting N2463 on a patrol of the Cambrai-Arras area, after flying from Biggin and refuelling at Merville. Because of his navigational experience, he often led these sweeps, but on this occasion was occupying the Red 2 slot in 'A' Flight, as the eleven green-and-brown warplanes went looking for trouble. They found it near Le Cateau as they prowled through banks of cumulus in open formation at 16,000 feet. Below were a number of specks which swiftly resolved into the slim shapes of around fifteen Dornier 17s of 1/KG77, and with whoops of pleasure the British pilots prepared to take full advantage of this gift. A sudden warning crackled in John's earphones, and he swivelled his head to see a dozen protecting Me 109s of JG2 diving on them from above and behind. It was his first sight of enemy fighters, and he pulled round hard to starboard and went into a full-throttle climb. A dark-camouflaged 109 appeared below him, also turning right. Almost subconsciously, Polly took the opportunity to fasten onto his opponent's tail as he emerged from his turn, and at 200 yards put some 400 rounds straight into the German fighter in a no-deflection shot. The Messerschmitt took no evasive action; with the pilot probably hit, it turned slowly over on its back like a dying fish, showing a pale blue belly, and slid into an inverted sixty-degree dive. Hurricane straining, John followed his victim down to 6,000 feet, but the 109, approaching terminal velocity, was impossible to catch. It was still on its back as it vanished into low cloud.

Abandoning the chase, he saw a Hurricane falling in a sheet of flame, accompanied by an open parachute. This was FO Milner, the first of 32's pilots to be shot down in battle. Seven 109s were

The Gloster Gauntlet II equipped 74 Squadron at Hornchurch from 1937 to the beginning of 1939. The main features of the machine can be appreciated in this photograph.

In February 1939, 74 became the fourth squadron to re-equip with the potent Spitfire I. This example has the two-blade propeller and flat cockpit hood of the earliest production machines, whilst an overzealous censor has seen fit to obliterate the serial number.

32 Squadron's dispersal hut at Biggin Hill, 1940. Note the aircraft recognition posters and the single pin-up to the left of the stove pipe. The pilots relaxed here between sorties. (J. Flinders)

Another room in the dispersal complex shows model-making activities. In the foreground, the pilots concentrate on the latest recognition sheets. (J. Flinders)

claimed in the whirling dogfight, including John's quarry. In ones and twos, the British fighters landed at St Omer to refuel before heading back to Merville and on to the Bump later in the evening.

For the next few days, 32 were engaged on sorties to the Lille-Arras-St Omer localities, usually refuelling at Hawkinge or Manston on the outward leg. On 23 May, John was leading a section of Hurricanes in N2527 over Bethune at 15,000 feet, when the aircraft ran into heavy and accurate anti-aircraft fire. A shell exploded close by him, rocking his fighter. He heard and felt shrapnel striking home, and a few minutes later his coolant temperature began rising ominously. By judiciously switching his Merlin on and off, he managed to coax the faltering N2527 towards the French coast. He reached the sea near Cap Gris Nez, identifying the lighthouse before he had to put down in a nearby field. His Hurricane was badly damaged in the heavy landing, but John emerged virtually unhurt.

French troops appeared from the lighthouse bearing the unpleasant, if inaccurate, news that the Germans were shooting all captured RAF aircrew out of hand. Not willing to test the truth of this possibility, and aware of enemy armour nearby, Polly headed for safety, thumbing a lift with a Belgian ambulance which took him to Boulogne. From there he was able to board a vessel which returned him to Southampton. Unfortunately he had been posted missing, believed killed, his companions assuming he was a 'goner' after witnessing the crash-landing. From Southampton he reached Waterloo, proceeding to Bromley South Station, where a nonchalant call to Biggin brought a car and an attractive WAAF, Isobel Clayton, to return him to base. John must have been impressed with the arrangements, as he later married his driver!

After a well-earned leave at his home in Chesterfield, Flinders returned to Biggin and 32's continuing round of patrols. His first, on 5 June in N2463, was cut short by low oil pressure, but he flew a number of other missions over France, often landing at French airfields to refuel. On the 8th, again in N2463, he was part of a squadron operation, accompanied by their sister unit 79, ordered to patrol Le Treport, to prevent the Luftwaffe harrying troop evacuations there. At 9.15 a.m. a formation of Heinkel IIIs, probably from KG1, were sighted 3,000 feet below, approaching in flights of three in line-astern. Crossley, the Red Leader, ordered sections line-astern, and the Hurricanes waded in. 32 did great execution among the enemy raiders, whilst 79 battled with their late-arriving escorts. One of the IIIs sent down was claimed by Polly, who, with the others, put down at Rouen Boos to refuel. In the event, they had to fly on to Dreux for petrol, and completed a second sortie over Fecamp before returning to their home airfield.

The squadron continued their tiring schedule daily across the Channel until mid-month, when their main ally capitulated, often completing several operational patrols a day, refuelling at Manston and ranging over Dieppe, Calais, Le Havre and St Valery. The sorties were usually armed reconnaissances, although on their last flight, on the 19th, they escorted Blenheims on a bombing raid to Amiens, with John flying N4260. By the 21st, 32 Squadron's participation in these operations was practically over. John only overflew the Continent once more that summer, accompanying Blenheims on a photographic reconnaissance sortie over St Valery and Berck-sur-Mer on the 20th of June, in N2577.

A new supply of raw pilots had been drafted in to join the unit, and they were in need of training in tactics and air discipline. Among them was Sergeant Pilot Burley Higgins from Whitwell, posted in at the end of June. Sadly, John never met him or flew with him in battle. In fact, by early July, Flinders had been given a new and onerous task; one that, to a great extent, was to keep him away from the day-to-day routine of a front-line fighter squadron. The Station Commander, Gp Capt. Grice, assigned him to the initial training of all new pilots drafted into 32. He was to teach the basics of formation flying, dog-fighting, attack strategy and tactics. John spent much of July and August inculcating the elements of fighter theory and practice to his students (who included several Poles), operating from an office and schoolroom on the south side of the airfield and commanding a training flight. He was allocated his own personal aircraft, a fairly clapped-out old warhorse, L2062, which had been passed on to 32 on 7 July. It was not all work – whenever possible he took off 'usually finding something to shoot at'.

On two occasions, Flinders engaged Heinkel IIIs, like the one depicted here. During one combat with the type, his armoured windscreen was damaged by a bullet strike from one of the bomber's beam guns.

John's greatest aerial success came on 18 August 1940, when he shot down two Messerschmitt 110C escorts in separate battles over Kent.

From early July, the '32nd Pursuit' – a nickname emulating United States Army Air Force parlance – were heavily engaged with the Luftwaffe, often operating from the forward Sector airfield at Hawkinge. John remained at Biggin, instilling the lessons of fighter airmanship into his charges. There were some compensations; he recalled happy, drunken nights at the White Hart in Brasted, the favourite watering-hole of so many of Biggin's fighter pilots during the war years. There were also trips to London's West End, wining and dining, and the crates of beer made available at dispersal by 'Groupy' Grice after a day of heavy fighting. 'Sleep', he remembered, 'was a rare commodity. There was too much to savour and live through, and tomorrow was another day.'

Polly found little time to indulge in his personal battle against Goering until 15 August. That evening, 32 Squadron and her new sister unit 610 took off to meet a two-pronged threat, with one point aimed at the Bump and a second which sneaked in to hit Croydon airport. John took off at 6.45 p.m. in his elderly and well-worn L2062, in company with Flt Lt 'Humph' Russell, who was intent on making up for lost time after spending some months in the Ops Room. The pair climbed hard towards Kenley, but Polly's flogged-out old Hurricane was outpaced and he lost his companion, who rapidly pulled away and disappeared. At 1,200 feet he saw shell-bursts pockmarking the sky over Croydon. He held his course in that direction, where rising clouds of smoke showed that the aerodrome was the raiders' target. At two o'clock, two Junkers 88s were 3,000 feet above, flying south-east around 4 miles away, and were obviously part of the bombing force. He turned in pursuit as they passed over Sevenoaks.

Left: *Squadron Leader Flinders in Canada in 1943.* (J. Flinders) Right: *In 1995 John posed for this shot, wearing the helmet and flying suit donated by Lt Horst Marx, whom he shot down over Frant on 15 August 1940.* (J. Flinders)

Slowly, Flinders' Hurricane, straining every rivet, was closing in on his prey when, at around 7.05 p.m., he saw the lean, bullet-shaped nose of an Me 109 approaching low from his right. Instinctively, he throttled his Merlin right back, laying off deflection as the enemy fighter crossed his sights from right to left. He was only some hundred yards away when he opened fire, seeing tracers from his two-second burst pierce the German's nose and lower cowling, bullets puncturing the glycol tank. Coolant streamed out, vaporising as it hit the air, pluming behind the Messerschmitt and marking the loss of the Daimler-Benz engine's very life-blood as it swiftly drained away. The German pilot, Lt Horst Marx, probably never even saw his victor as he headed home in his E-4 of 3/Erpr.Gr.210. As the thickening white trail gushed away behind his quarry, John realised 'he could not get home' and pulled away towards his original targets, spotting a parachute blossom at 6,000 feet away to the south of Sevenoaks as his victim baled out. The doomed Messerschmitt hit the ground in flames at Lightland Farm, Frant, at 7.10 p.m., with its pilot escaping successfully. The crash site has been investigated and the fighter's compass is on display in the Robertsbridge Aviation Society's museum. Flinders was still hopeful of catching the fleeing Junkers, but the 109's involuntary sacrifice had saved them. He saw them again, but by this time they were 6 miles away. At the coast, with the bandits well on their way home, he gave them best and turned away for base.

Later that same evening, John was enjoying a few well-deserved beers in the mess with other 32 Squadron pilots, when the Intelligence Officer appeared with a young Luftwaffe pilot who, he said, wished to be introduced to the flier who had shot him down an hour or so earlier. Lt Marx clicked heels as he was presented and insisted on handing over his flying suit, lifejacket and helmet to a bemused Flinders. These prized items are still kept by John's son in Canada.

John's most successful battle with the Luftwaffe came three days later, on a warm, peaceful Sunday afternoon. The sirens began wailing soon after lunch, as several large enemy formations were tracked crossing south-east England, headed towards London. The first target was Kenley to the south-west, and a 50-plus plot over Tunbridge Wells was almost certainly aimed at the Bump. With twelve minutes to go before the bombers appeared overhead, the attack alarm was sounded, and 32 and 610 were scrambled. Minutes after the snarling departure of the two squadrons, the sudden quiet was broken by the unmistakeable crackle of a single Merlin, as Polly's lone L2062 taxied from the maintenance hangars and took off with a healthy roar. The time was exactly 1 p.m.

The Derbyshire pilot climbed hard to 12,000 feet with the throttle wide open, where he met the twelve Hurricanes of his own squadron and tagged on at the rear. At 1.20 p.m. a strung-out gaggle of enemy aircraft around thirty strong hove in sight 3,000 feet above, approaching from the south-east. The fleet of twin-engined, twin-finned raiders were first identified as Dornier 17s, and the initial attack sent them scattering in all directions. They were, in fact, Messerschmitt 110Cs of ZG26 on escort duty. John came in behind one of the dark-painted *Zerstörers*, with the luminous bars on his reflector framing its 53-foot wingspan at 200 yards, as his eight machine guns delivered four concentrated bursts. Over 2,000 rounds of ammunition flayed the fragile aluminium skin of the 110, which gushed flame and smoke as it rolled away beyond the vertical, plummeting straight down to smash violently into the ground near Godstone. The unfortunate crew, Fw. Klare and Uffz. Brugner, were never found, presumably blown to shreds along with their disintegrated warplane.

Pulling away and circling in a rapidly clearing sky, John picked out another twin-engined aircraft heading east at 12,000 feet, and turned to pursue. The machine was an Me 110C-2 of 1/ZG26, but again, in the stress and excitement of battle, he mistook it for a Dornier '215', falling behind it in a hard stern-chase and flogging his game old veteran to get within range. Polly knew he was short of ammunition, and was determined to get near enough to use his remaining rounds to best effect. The 'Dornier' dived groundwards, levelling out at 3,000 feet with his pursuer gradually closing in. The chase lasted for around 40 miles, passing north of West Malling, where airmen frantically waved and cheered him on, then over Detling, with Flinders then only 600 yards away.

In *The Hardest Day*, Alfred Price records that the 12th Light Anti-Aircraft Regiment at Dunkirk radar station west of Canterbury, fired forty-seven 40mm shells at the 110, perceptibly slowing it with hits on the wings and empennage. John totally rejected this view, calling it 'nonsense, as far as I am concerned'. His thesis was that by the time hunter and hunted had passed north of Canterbury he would be so close – 'right up his tail' as he put it – that any ack-ack fire would have hit him as well as his target. Below 200 feet and 2 miles north of the cathedral city, the 110 had to pull out of its gradual dive, and as it did so lost speed, allowing the tenacious Polly to close his juddering fighter to within 150 yards of his prey. Triggering a final four-second burst that exhausted his ammunition, his concentrated fire chewed up the Messerschmitt's fuselage and starboard motor. The DB601 caught fire, and the escort fighter reeled to the left, hitting the ground at Rough Common, Harbledown, and disintegrating in a fierce explosion which hurled fragments in all directions. The impact was so violent that no trace of the crewmen, Uffzs Mai and Gebauer, was ever found. It had been a hard chase, but John's determination and the gallant response of his old warhorse had gained him two final and well-authenticated kills.

John only met the enemy in the air once more, on a patrol off Newcastle as Blue Leader in N3679 on 26 September, when 32 were resting at Acklington. His section aimed a few bursts at a Heinkel III which escaped in heavy cloud. He remained with the 32nd Pursuit for seven more months, before a posting to No.55 OTU at Aston Down. In late March 1941, he married his WAAF driver, Isobel, at Box in Wiltshire. Both their children, a son and daughter, later emigrated to live in Canada.

From No.55 OTU, John served with several non-operational units. These included two spells at No.2 Fighter Instruction School at Montrose where, in the spring of 1943, he was in charge of 'F' Flight, operating Miles Master trainers. As Ray Holmes explained in his book, *Sky Spy*, there was fierce competition between the eight flights, four deploying Airspeed Oxford twin-engined trainers and four flying Masters. Flying officially started at 8 a.m., and the objective was to be airborne as soon after this as possible. To steal a march on his fellow flight commanders, Polly always arranged overnight inspections on the two aircraft normally flown by his flight. This meant that they were warmed up and ready by 7.55 a.m., already taxiing to the flight hut door, where there were already pupil pilots in the cockpit. At eight on the dot, both his instructors were strapped in the back seats of the Masters, and both trainers were invariably first off the ground each day.

However, one morning another Master flight, accompanied by two Oxfords, decided to try the same trick, and all six aeroplanes met on the runway, jostling for take-off positions. John was not amused, and the following day he put into practice his own solution. His fellow 'F' Flight instructors, like himself ex-fighter pilots accustomed to scrambles, formed up with him in vic at dispersal and taxied onto the runway. Superior numbers persuaded their rivals not to dispute possession, and all three trainers roared into the air in a tight V formation. It was later revealed that the racket caused by the trio of Masters snarling low over the rooftops of Montrose at full throttle roused many citizens from their beds and brought others to their doors. All three miscreants were duly carpeted by the Station CO, Wg Cdr Scott, albeit with a twinkle in his eye. He applauded the 'good show' but feared a multiple prang in the town market place if emulated by other flights. With a huge grin, he forthwith banned formation take-offs, but he had clearly enjoyed the joke.

John also completed the Empire Central Flying School course at Hullavington. This was designed for long-service regular RAF officers and covered advanced training in ground subjects, plus experience on a variety of aircraft types. It was good preparation for his posting to Canada on the liner *Empress of Scotland* in May 1943, where for two years he was seconded to the RCAF at their CFS at Trenton, Ontario.

For the whole of this period, John was one of two flying members, with the eventual rank of squadron leader, of the Examining Flight, whose responsibility was to assess the air and ground training standards of all the Dominion Flying Schools. To eliminate any possibility of influence on their assessments, they were forbidden to stay overnight on any bases, but were allowed the best local hotels and their own Lockheed Electra for transport. John recalled it as an interesting, though demanding, assignment, during which he had the opportunity to see most of Canada. He returned to England on the prestigious troop transport *Queen Elizabeth* in March 1945, but by this time he had decided that the peacetime RAF was not for him. He refused a permanent commission, and was released into the Reserve in November of that year. Polly joined the Firestone Tyre Company in 1946 as a sales representative. By 1948 he was the South-West Regional Manager at Bristol, and on his retirement twenty years later he had risen to the position of Firestone UK General Manager, in charge of sales and exports. He and Isobel emigrated that year to join their children who were living in Canada.

Like other worthy Derbyshire airmen, John received no decorations for his gallant service, nor for his status as a fighter ace. Graham Wallace wrote in his *RAF Biggin Hill* that the 1940 Station CO, Gp Capt. Grice, was ever keen to ensure that his pilots received due credit for their success. 'The surest way to incur the Station Commander's wrath', he commented, 'was to keep him in ignorance when a pilot had scored his fifth victory. Then he would at once send a recommendation for an immediate award to Headquarters Fighter Command.' Whether someone nodded on the job and failed to inform 'Groupy' of his score is not known, but John Layton Flinders remains one of the very few officer pilots with up to six-plus combat kills not to wear the ribbon of the Distinguished Flying Cross. His hard work was also apparently unappreciated, both in Great Britain and Canada, on behalf of the many pupil pilots who came under his aegis. Many training staff were awarded the OBE or AFC for services such as those he rendered to the RAF and RCAF.

During his Royal Air Force career, John, who died in June 1998, in his eighty-first year, completed over 2,600 hours in the air, and his final flying assessment was, like the man himself, rated as 'exceptional'.

six

Squadron Leader
Henry Collingham Baker

Combat Record

Date	Sqn	Locality	Aircraft Flown	Enemy type	Claim
01.06.40	19	Dunkirk	Spitfire I L1030	Messerschmitt 110C	Destroyed
				Messerschmitt 110C	Damaged
15.09.40	41	Foulness	Spitfire I R6697	Heinkel IIIH	Destroyed (shared)
		S. of London		Heinkel IIIH	Damaged
30.09.40	41	S.W. of Dungeness	Spitfire I X4052	Messerschmitt 109E	Destroyed
01.11.40	421 Flt	E. of Margate	Hurricane IIA L.Z–T	Messerschmitt 109E	Destroyed
24.11.40	421 Flt	S.E. of Dungeness	Spitfire IIA L.Z-O	Messerschmitt 109E	Destroyed (shared)
				Messerschmitt 109E	Damaged
26.05.41	74	S. of Dover	Spitfire IIA P8388	Messerschmitt 109F	Destroyed
12.10.42	229	N. of Malta	Spitfire VC	Messerschmitt 109F	Damaged
13.10.42	229	Kalafrana Bay	Spitfire VC	Messerschmitt 109F	Damaged

A portrait of Pilot Officer Henry Collingham Baker in 1940. (H.C. Baker)

Squadron Leader Henry Collingham Baker

HARRY BAKER was one of three noted Second World War fighter pilots who hailed from the Chesterfield area, following in the footsteps of two who served in the First World War. Two of the three were educated at the local grammar school, and all three enlisted as career airmen and fought in the Battle of Britain. Baker, the youngest of the trio, was born in Clowne (a subject of wry amusement to him throughout life) in May 1920, as the only child of Joseph Herbert and Frances Baker. His father was a schoolmaster who became head of Creswell Senior School before the Second World War. Harry's middle name, Collingham, was that of his mother before her marriage.

Baker attended Chesterfield and Mansfield Grammar Schools before completing his studies at King's College, Taunton. He joined the RAF as a regular in July 1938, receiving his *ab initio* tuition at No.9 EFTS at Ansty, before progressing to Uxbridge for kitting-out and recruit training; in September, he was posted to No.9 FTS at Hullavington. With his flying training completed, Harry spent five months from May to September 1939 at No.1 Electrical and Wireless School, Cranwell, as a staff pilot. He was posted to 616 Squadron, AAF at the outbreak of war, then non-operational on Gauntlets, before moving on to 19 Squadron at Duxford via the 12 Group Pool at Aston Down. The unit operated Spitfire Is, having been the first RAF squadron to equip with the type in August 1938. Attached to 'B' Flight, Harry speedily took to this outstanding aircraft, gaining valuable experience through many flying hours in the winter and early spring of the Phoney War. Whilst at Duxford he recalls being delegated to check out Douglas Bader on a Spitfire before the latter's first flight on the type. Harry was the 'young lad of twenty' – nineteen in fact – rather disparagingly referred to by Paul Brickhill in *Reach for the Sky*:

> *The boy prattled on about R/T procedure, making it seem so complicated that Bader impatiently cut him short … [Baker] had omitted to tell him that the undercarriage always hung on the withdrawal pins and a couple of pumps removed the weight of the wheels and allowed the selector freedom to travel into the 'down' position.*

Not surprisingly, Harry's recollection of the event differed slightly from that described by the author.

Harry went into action with 19 Squadron for the first time on 1 June in 1940. Now based at Hornchurch, the unit had been patrolling over Dunkirk since 26 May as part of a massive Fighter Command effort aimed at keeping the Luftwaffe off the backs of the hard-pressed BEF, as the Navy struggled to rescue them from the open beaches. 19 were part of the newly-formed Hornchurch Wing, which included 41 and 222, plus 616 who flew from the satellite airfield at Rochford. 1 June was destined to be the RAF's busiest day during the whole of Operation Dynamo, and the Wing lifted off at 4.20 a.m., crossing the French coast at 5 a.m. on an offensive sortie. Harry flew Spitfire L1030 in Green Section, keeping careful lookout as the squadron, led by Flt Lt Brian 'Sandy' Lane patrolled the coastline 3 miles north-east of the beleaguered port, its position easily identified by the thick smudges of black smoke rising from the burning oil tanks. At 5.40 a.m., as 19 prowled among thickening cloud at 4,000 feet, the shapes of five wicked-looking Messerschmitt 109s appeared ahead, diving out of the murk in front of the leading section. Lane called for sections line-astern, and immediately afterwards four twin-motor Me 110s came into sight from the landward side. More followed, and Baker looked around for a suitable target as 19 went into the attack.

Glancing upward, he saw a slender silhouette some thousand feet above and to his left, with the twin fins and engines establishing it as another 110. Opening his throttle, the 1,000hp of his racing Merlin pulled him up towards his quarry. Pushing the glowing ring of his reflector in front of the Messerschmitt's nose, he fired a long deflection shot, seeing the tracer from his eight Brownings flying into or around the bandit before he had to pull away to avoid a collision. He did not see what happened to the 110, but reported 'it was waffling badly' as he broke.

No sooner had Harry snapped off a quick burst at a second 110 without apparent effect, than a third *Zerstörer* appeared, turning into him with bright flashes winking from its nose as the enemy pilot opened up. Squeezing his own gun button, the Derbyshire pilot took his opponent head-on, seeing his own fire strike as the two-seater flashed underneath him, both motors gushing white vapour. Baker turned rapidly in pursuit, boring in closely behind the Messerschmitt and flailing it from short range with his second burst of fire. The enemy fighter immediately burst into flames, falling out of the sky in front of him like a blazing comet. Convinced of his target's destruction Harry pulled away, seeing more 110s ahead gyrating in a defensive circle. He fired an optimistic burst, 'certain I didn't get anywhere near them'. A group of specks materialised rapidly to starboard, resolving into the shark-like shapes of Me 109s. Short of fuel and ammunition, he took refuge in a layer of cloud and came home alone to be granted a Messerschmitt 110 destroyed and a second damaged. It is worth noting that Brian Lane felt the 110 crews to be tyros. In his book *Spitfire!*, he wrote:

> ... *by our standards of training these pilots should never have left FTS, yet here they were, trying to fight four times their number and with no idea of how to do it ... Even as I cursed, I realised what a queer thought this was. We ought to be thankful for cold meat like this.*

Harry left 19 Squadron in late June and after a spell in hospital as the result of a road accident, he was posted to 41 Squadron at Hornchurch in August. He made his second combat claim whilst flying with this unit on Sunday 15 September, which was later designated Battle of Britain Day. The day before had been set aside for his wedding, but the marriage had to be deferred when he was hurriedly recalled from leave. After a heavy morning attack on London had been repulsed, the Luftwaffe returned that afternoon, sending massive formations spread across a ten-mile front and approaching the capital shortly after 2.00 p.m. 41 Squadron were one of the many units scrambled to meet this threat, with Harry piloting Spitfire R6697 in 'A' Flight. The squadron were at 20,000 feet by 2.30 p.m., looking down on a vast phalanx of Heinkel IIIs which were 6,000 feet below and screened by numerous 109s. The Spitfires manoeuvred into line-astern, and Baker heard the 'Tally Ho' on his R/T. At that moment he looked up and saw a formation of 109s just above; he swung his fighter up to attack.

As he closed on the rearmost aircraft, Harry attempted too tight a turn in the rarefied air and spun away, pulling out some way below. Levelling his skittish warplane, he found himself on a collision course with a mass of Heinkels. Gently easing back his control column, he flew down one line-astern column of bombers, passing over each aircraft and hammering out a burst as it came on through his GM2 gunsight. The last raider ran into a converging stream of tracer at 100 yards, which disappeared into its streamlined nose and front fuselage before Harry pushed his stick forward, passing underneath his target and straight into cloud. He later wrote of this attack that after recovering from the spin:

> *I saw a formation of Heinkels beneath me and in front coming head-on. My first reaction was to do as much damage as I possibly could. I flew across the top of them, pressing the tit as soon as one came into my sight. I was not worried about the escorts, as they were too high to interfere. I kept going straight on, and saw my rounds hitting the nose of the Heinkel at the rear of the formation, and continued my dive underneath it.*

With some two-thirds of his ammunition expended, Baker searched for further prey, descending to 1,500 feet in the Southend locality. There, at 3.30 p.m., he picked up trade in the shape of a lone Heinkel IIIH-4 under assault from two Hurricanes, probably from 257 and 310 Squadrons. As they pulled away he bored in from astern, loosing a six-second burst from 100 yards away, closing to point-blank range and expending all his rounds. Smoke pumped from the raider's port engine, and as his bullets smashed the hydraulics, both landing wheels swung down from their nacelles. By this time the hard-hit Heinkel was low down and well east of Southend. As Baker circled, the enemy pilot put his riddled aeroplane down on a mud-bank at St Asplen's Head, Foulness. The crew struggled from the bomber, a 1/KG26 machine (Wn 6985, and coded '1H+1H'), which was a complete write-off. In recent years some wreckage has been recovered, including an undercarriage leg, wheel and tyre. These items were passed on to the Kent Battle of Britain Museum and are now preserved by the Hawkinge Aeronautical Trust. He claimed a half-share of one Heinkel and damage to a second.

Two days later, 41 were embroiled in an afternoon dogfight over the Kent coast with 109s of JG53. Four of the unit's Spitfires were damaged to some extent, and Harry was caught up in a confused and fast-moving all-fighter combat. He scored hits on one Messerschmitt and was levelling out to engage a second, when he glimpsed another on his tail. His fighter, serialled X4409, a brand-new machine delivered only five days earlier, had its Merlin knocked out and he had to make a speedy decision whether to bale out or attempt a forced landing. A glance out of the cockpit showed him 'it was a bloody long way down' and he decided to stick with his machine, gliding down to a wheels-up landing near the village of Stelling Minnis, south of Canterbury. As his Spitfire ploughed its way across a field, he lost part of the tail unit and gashed his forehead on the gunsight. Unfortunately his parents were informed that he was missing and spent an anxious day or two before learning he was safe.

Harry Baker had to postpone his wedding, which was scheduled for 15 September 1940, due to more pressing engagements. He finally married Betty Todd at Gainsborough on 8 October. (H.C. Baker)

Baker's first kill was a Messerschmitt 110C, which was one of two claims he made over Dunkirk on 1 June 1940, while flying with 19 Squadron.

Baker met the formidable Messerschmitt 109 on a number of occasions. His combat claims included three of the breed, plus shares in two others.

A friendly farmer patched up Harry's wound and fed him, and the Derbyshire flier set off to return to base. He reached Central London by the evening, and a motorist dropped him off at one of the big hotels, where he was spotted by Helen Kilpatrick, a staff reporter from the *Chicago Daily News*. 'His entrance was, to say the least, sensational', she gushed in her later report.

The swinging door revolved and into the brilliant light walked a young RAF pilot with parachute harness, flying boots and gear. He had a deep cut down his forehead. Quickly a crowd gathered round but he made for a group captain in one corner. Later I was invited to join them in the bar, and his story came out.

The following morning she was told he had rejoined his squadron.

Harry gained his revenge on 30 September, when 41 formed part of a force intercepting a heavy raid launched over the Sussex coast towards London, just after midday. He was flying X4052 and was detached by his CO on a reconnaissance, climbing to 25,000 feet where he sighted a cluster of twin-engined aircraft around 10,000 feet below. He reported the enemy formation to Control, then received a disagreeable surprise as an Me 109 hurtled past him in a dive to starboard, its square-cut wings and braced tailplanes standing out clearly as it went by, apparently without seeing him. Glancing upwards, Baker was even more disturbed to see a further fifty-plus 109s swarming about at 28,000 feet 'in no formation at all'. Seeing his lone Spitfire below, five of the single-seaters broke away to attack, and he had to dive away, plunging into a layer of cloud to escape their attentions. After a few minutes' wait he emerged below cloud to find himself alone.

Baker continued his patrol, flying out across the Channel, and at 1.50 p.m., 10 miles south-west of Dungeness, he saw a lone Me 109 heading for home, a faint trace of glycol issuing from an obvious coolant leak. He pushed X4052's nose down in a swift dive on his opponent, loosing off a short burst at 400 yards, cursing as the 109 pilot saw him and dodged away seawards. Fastening on to the German's tail, he fired the remainder of his 2,800 rounds in a long, continuous burst, closing in to the killing range of fifty yards and seeing his victim plummet into the sea, disappearing in a geyser of climbing spray. Two boats pulled towards the crash site, which probably marked the demise of a 109 flown by Uffz. Vogel of 6/JG53. His fighter, Wn 6384 and coded 3+-, was shot down into the sea off Beachy head at that time, while returning from a bomber escort mission with a malfunctioning engine, which probably explains the trail of coolant vapour. The pilot was rescued and was made a prisoner of war.

The Derbyshire aviator finally made it to his wedding on 8 October, at Gainsborough Parish Church, where he married Betty Todd, who worked at a local bank. The ceremony was performed by the vicar of Elmton and Creswell and the rector of Duckmanton. According to the *Derbyshire Times*, Harry brought a mascot with him – a small, silky-haired dog rescued from a bombed house in London, whose occupants had all been killed. After the reception Harry and Betty drove away for a honeymoon in the south of England.

He was on the move again in that same month, being posted as a flying officer to a new hush-hush unit formed at Gravesend on 7 October at the personal instigation of Winston Churchill. 421 Flight was created from a nucleus of 66 Squadron pilots, and used that unit's code letters, 'L' and 'Z', on its aircraft, but with a hyphen between the two letters (L-Z). Harry may have owed his move to his individualistic streak. On several occasions he had attacked German formations on his own, and his leader had detached him on 30 September on a solo recce way above the rest of the squadron. The keynote of the new element was individuality, and the 'Jim Crow' flight's main duties were patrol sorties over the coasts of England and Northern France, looking for incoming raids which RDF could not pick up. They also reported on the movements of enemy aircraft, their camouflage and combat tactics. Originally they flew solo, but early losses dictated a change of strategy, and they soon began operating in pairs.

421 began operations with six new-model Spitfire IIs, powered by 1,175hp Merlin XIIs. On 12 October these were supplemented by ten Hurricane IIAs powered by 1,200hp Merlin XXs fitted

with two-stage blowers – among the first Mk II Hurricanes ever delivered, and the fastest of all the Hurricane variants. In early November, at the instigation of the CO, Flt Lt Charles 'Paddy' Green, nine more Spitfire IIs joined the flight, though one might have thought the unit would have operated better with one type of fighter, rather than two. Harry had his first action with his new mixed force on 20 October, when he had to hide in cloud to evade around twenty Me 109s who attacked him while on patrol. On the 30th, 421 moved to West Malling, and he experienced his first combat with them on 1 November.

According to the Flight's ORB, Baker piloted Hurricane L.Z-T on this occasion, flying a lone spotter patrol over the coast at 25,000 feet through five-tenths of cloud. Although he flew both types of fighter deployed by the unit, he preferred the Spitfire. In the latter he always felt himself an integral part of the machine, whereas in a Hurricane he had the distinct impression he was 'sitting on top of it'. Soon after 2 p.m., a formation of nine Me 109s appeared above and ahead. He followed them, climbing and loosing off a few speculative bursts at 250 yards without apparent effect. By this time he was 25 miles east of Margate, and was distracted by a series of white columns spouting up from the distant sea below. His immediate thought was that he was witnessing an enemy attack on shipping, and sure enough he identified some thirty-six Dornier 17s in vics of three below him, protected by around 40 Me 109s operating in two groups of 20. The bombers were 'milling around', apparently attacking a convoy. Harry lost height in a gentle dive, hoping for a chance to engage the nearest Messerschmitt. He launched a beam attack, seeing his tracer strike the 109 in the belly before it broke away. It was clearly hit but he was unable to see what happened to it.

By now around 5,000 feet above the waters of the Channel, he sighted another 109 pulling out of a strafing run. Like its companions, it had a bright yellow nose and wingtips. Fastening on to this unsuspecting target, he flayed it with his remaining ammunition, closing to his customary point-blank range from above and behind, and saw the fire from his close-grouped Brownings tearing into the enemy's cockpit. With the pilot obviously dead, the Messerschmitt nosed over into a vertical dive and smashed straight into the water, down to the distant sea bed, with only a transitory plume of spray to mark its passage. Baker wave-hopped back to base, claiming one victim down in the sea and a second Messerschmitt probably destroyed.

Single patrol activity continued throughout the month, and on 24 November he piloted Spitfire L.Z-O on a mid-afternoon shipping recce from Hawkinge. Towards the end of his beat, flying at 27,000 feet, he was vectored on to a ten-plus raid which he intercepted around 30 miles due north of Dungeness. As he approached he saw a squadron of friendly fighters – Hurricanes from 501 – breaking up the enemy force of about fifteen Me 109s. The German fighters dived away steeply under the Hurricanes' attack, heading for the Kent coast. Scenting another kill, Harry dived his Spitfire at full boost, intent on the chase. He had been specialising in the clinical despatch of single 109s, shot down in solitary attacks from behind – classic lone-wolf tactics, hitting an enemy who never even saw him - and the covey of plunging warplanes ahead provided obvious candidates to help increase his score.

He caught up the rearmost Messerschmitt at around 2,000 feet before it crossed the coast, opening fire at 400 yards with slight deflection. As Harry closed, he glimpsed two more aircraft ahead of his quarry, both in rough line-astern. His eight wing-guns rattled out a prolonged five-second burst, at which the leading fighter of the trio now ahead of him began to vomit a thickening mist of coolant. At the same time the aircraft behind it turned steeply and shot past his Spitfire, back towards the English coast. He had a momentary thought that this aeroplane might have been a Hurricane, breaking off after hitting the 109 ahead of it, when he saw other unidentified fighters closing in behind him. As the 'Hurricane' disappeared astern, Harry saw the crippled 109 plunge into the Channel 3 miles south-east of Dungeness, a demise later confirmed by the Folkestone Police. Only his original target now remained in front of him, and he strove to close the range, spraying it with tracer which he saw hitting home but doing no apparent vital damage. The last of his ammunition now expended, marked by the clatter of empty breechblocks, a frustrated Baker

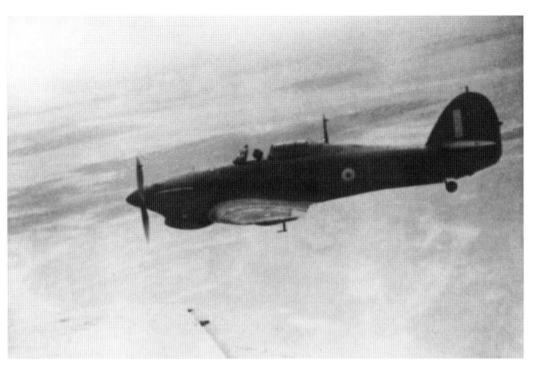

Baker served with 127 Squadron in the Western Desert during 1942. He is shown here piloting one of the unit's Hurricane IIBs. Note the drag-inducing Vokes air filter under the nose of the fighter. (H.C. Baker)

Harry commanded 229 Squadron in Malta late in 1942, flying Spitfire VCs similar to EP257, which is shown running up on one of the island's airfields. Again, notice how the air filter spoils the clean lines of the warplane. (H.C. Baker)

pulled away and left his antagonist to live another day. After due consideration, he thought the aircraft he had taken for a Hurricane might have been a third 109, and the German fighter which went into the sea might have been his own victim, which he had involuntarily hit by using too much deflection in his opening bursts. Such things were not unknown. He was awarded a conservative claim of half a 109 destroyed, shared with 501 Squadron, plus a damaged, giving him a total score of three kills, two further shared victories, and three damaged.

'Butch' Baker remained with 421 Flight until December 1940. In the New Year he was posted, after a short spell on loan to 306 (Polish) Squadron at Tern Hill, to 'B' Flight 74 Squadron, then at Biggin Hill under the command of the legendary 'Sailor' Malan. The unit was just going over to the offensive over France, organising itself for a programme of sweeps – 'circuses, rhubarbs and ramrods' – in support of the new RAF policy of penetrating German-held airspace and trying to provoke the Luftwaffe into giving battle. In retrospect, a better policy might have been to send some of the Spitfire squadrons tied up in this strategy to assist hard-pressed Malta and the fighter units in the Western Desert, who were struggling with their outmoded fighter equipment. Harry regarded his sojourn with 74 as the happiest period of all his wartime RAF service, often flying as wingman to the CO, and becoming a friend and admirer of Malan's successor, John Mungo-Park. Harry flew several missions from various bases without getting to close quarters with the German air force until the end of May.

229 Squadron Spitfire Vs line up at Qrendi, north of Luqa, late in 1942. The nearest aircraft is EP641 (X-J). While on the island all 229s warplanes were coded 'X' rather than the official designation HB.
(H.C. Baker)

On the 26th of that month he led Green Section on a 'rhubarb', piloting Spitfire IIA P8388. He took off from Gravesend with his number two, PO Sandman, in P7782 at 3.15 p.m., winging low over the Channel towards Boulogne. After half-an-hour's flying, an Me 109F was spotted heading towards England, and both Spitfires turned in pursuit. The German fighter dodged into cloud and Green Section resumed its mission. With cloud thickening over the French coast, the weather was judged too dangerous for low flying, so the section turned back for base. As Baker and his wingman approached Dover at 4.10 p.m., the leader saw the harbour barrage balloons under attack, with one blazing inflatable drifting down through the sky like a huge flying whale on fire. He sighted a 109, which had evidently shot-up the balloon and was probably the machine they had seen over the Channel. Harry attacked from astern, at around 500 feet over the sea, getting in a very brief burst before the Messerschmitt broke away and disappeared. As he glanced round rapidly to relocate it, his adversary reappeared behind him, opening fire from dead astern. In his turn Baker took violent evasive action, steep-turning so hard to avoid the German's tracer that he blacked out.

As his vision cleared, Harry realised his manoeuvre had brought him directly behind his foe, who was now just ahead and slightly to port, doubtless wondering where the Spitfire had gone. He was soon in no doubt, for with P8388 in the perfect firing position, Harry lined the 32-foot wingspan of his slim target in his range-bars at 100 yards distance, and saw his eight machine guns tear chunks of metal from the 109's airframe. After four seconds, the stricken fighter rolled to starboard and disappeared. Baker reported it down in the sea some 3 miles south of the Kentish port, but the Messerschmitt seemed to have struggled back to nearby France, where it crash-landed at Ligescourt. The 1/JG53 machine, Wn 5734, suffered some forty per cent battle damage in the encounter, being fairly well wrecked. This kill gave Harry ace status, taking the Derbyshire fighter pilot's score beyond five, with three-and-a-half of them being the vaunted German single-seaters built at Augsberg.

The powers-that-be must have felt Harry Baker was in need of a rest because in August he was moved on to training duties at 52 OTU at Debden, followed by a spell with No.5 at Aston Down, away from the front line in rural Gloucestershire. By April 1942, he had become a flight lieutenant and was operational again, flying Hurricane IIBs with 127 Squadron in the Western Desert, although he did not meet the Axis in the air. He recalled that during this time he shared a tent with Ian Smith, the future prime minister of Southern Rhodesia. Remaining in the Mediterranean theatre, he was promoted to acting squadron leader to head 229 Squadron, flying Spitfire VCs on Malta. Colin Parkinson, an Australian fighter pilot serving on the island, remembered 'Butch' Baker as 'a good type'. He led the unit for a month and was involved in several interceptions during October. On the afternoon of the 12th, he led eight Spitfires in an attack on Messerschmitt 109Fs protecting an incoming raid north of Malta, scoring strikes on one escort. The following afternoon 229 caught up with a seventy-plus enemy formation over Kalafrana Bay. The CO damaged a 109 of 1/JG77, which was his final combat claim. Harry never felt he did himself justice as commander of 229 Squadron, which is hardly surprising as he was by this time a sick and exhausted man. Under pressure from a combination of malaria and dysentery, he relinquished his leadership later that month and spent some time recuperating at the military hospital in St Paul's Bay, reverting to his previous rank.

By the early part of 1943, Harry was back in England, where he was given a choice of postings – one as a test pilot, another as OC Tactics and Training at HQ Northern Ireland. The latter job would give him his half-ring back, so he chose it. He admits it was an unwise decision. After three months he was moved to 55 OTU, Annan, followed in May by a spell on the Gibraltar-Cairo run, helping to ferry 300 Hurricanes to the Russians. His final tour of operational duty was as a supernumerary flight lieutenant with 118 Squadron in the latter months of 1943, piloting fairly venerable Spitfire VBs, first at Coltishall, but eventually suffering banishment to the far north of Scotland. During 1944 he spent his time as a ferry pilot at Croydon; at the CFS, Montrose, on an instructor's course; and on a posting to Wrexham as Chief Flying Instructor. In January 1945 he was appointed as Chief Ground Instructor at No.17 FTS at Cranwell, and ended his service career as a squadron leader at Kimbolton in command of the recruits' training wing. Somewhat disillusioned, he decided not to pursue a career in the post-war RAF, and was demobilised in January 1946.

Harry Baker's subsequent career was both colourful and successful. In 1946 he took his wife and young son, Michael (who was born in 1944 and later became an RAF officer), to Ceylon where he tried his hand at tea-planting. In 1948 he went to Peru, where he worked for the state railways until 1953, and was certain he met the war criminal Klaus Barbie. That year he joined a Grimsby company operating a fleet of cargo vessels. Harry quickly developed an expertise in commerce and export, which earned him the accolade of 'one of Humberside's leading shipping men'. He retired in 1985 as managing director of Norcargo Ltd, a busy and successful company which operated its own cargo terminal at the port. His wife, Betty, who died in 1975, established her own gown shop in the town.

Like his Chesterfield compatriots, 'Butch' was a skilful and noted flier, who displayed keenness and determination in an operational career which took him from England to the Middle East, and which resulted in the destruction of at least five enemy aircraft, with no less than five others damaged. Like 'Polly' Flinders, he received no official recognition for his contribution to the defeat of the Luftwaffe, which was another inexplicable and unjust oversight by his superiors. Harry, who possesses a quiet sense of humour as well as a keen business acumen, retired to Cleethorpes on the Lincolnshire coast, but still vividly remembers the days when he was 'One of the Few'. Modestly he feels his service has received too much exposure, and that 'people are getting a bit fed up reading about it'. Fortunately his opinion is not shared by the many who continue to respect the dwindling band of heroes like himself, who gave us our first glimpses of hope during the dark early years of the Second World War.

seven

Sergeant Pilot
William Burley Higgins

Combat Record

Date	Sqn	Locality	Aircraft Flown	Enemy Type	Claim
03.07.40	32	Baybrooks, Horsmonden	Hurricane I N2670	Dornier 17Z	Destroyed (shared)
20.07.40	32	Dover	Hurricane I P3679	Messerschmitt 110C	Destroyed
12.08.40	32	Dover	Hurricane I N2524	Messerschmitt 109E	Destroyed
24.08.40	32	Folkestone	Hurricane I P3679	Messerschmitt 109E	Destroyed
11.09.40	253	Lewes Thames Estuary	Hurricane I R2686	Messerschmitt 109E Messerschmitt 110C	Destroyed Damaged

Sergeant William Burley Higgins in December 1939 at No.5 FTS, Sealand. (D. Higgins)

Sergeant Pilot William Burley Higgins

WILLIAM BURLEY HIGGINS, always known as 'Burley' to friends and relatives, was born in September 1913 at Belph, Hodthorpe, near Whitwell in the extreme north-east of the county. He was the eldest of nine children and was educated at Brunts Grammar School in Mansfield. He was a keen and successful sportsman and wished to become a teacher, spening seven months during 1932/33 as an uncertified teacher at his old school, Whitwell Senior, before joining Culham College at Abingdon in August 1934 for a two-year training course. At Culham he spent many hours participating in sporting activities and was vice-captain of the soccer XI. His final college report of August 1936 described him as 'a fine, athletic Englishman; open-air type, kindly and good-natured'. Burley returned from Culham to the post of handicrafts teacher at his former school, where he taught until the outbreak of the Second World War.

Burley Higgins was well known and popular in the district, excelling at football and cricket – he was locally renowned as a punishing left-hand bat – and was a natural shot, an essential attribute for an intending fighter pilot. His keen eye was also evident when playing darts, where he could unerringly score doubles and trebles with notable skill. He joined the RAFVR in 1937, the year following its formation, learning to fly basic trainers at Tollerton Airfield near Nottingham. He soloed before the war began, and immediately after his six-week ordeal of recruit training at No.4 ITW, Bexhill-on-Sea was behind him, he reported to No.5 FTS at Sealand near Chester, joining No.45 Course in December 1939. By the following June his airmanship had been rated as 'Considerably Above the Average', as he passed out on the advanced Miles Master I monoplane trainer. The only modern fighter aeroplane to visit Sealand was Hurricane N2387, whose call provided 45 Course with their only opportunity to see a front-line interceptor at close quarters. These rugged, reliable machines – the first of the eight-gun RAF warplanes – were destined to be the mainstay of Fighter Command throughout 1940.

No.45 Course passed out before the OTUs were established, although the need for them was becoming clearly apparent. Single-engine graduates were posted directly to operational squadrons without the benefit of specific air-combat training, and many met their deaths at the hands of the enemy within a few weeks. After a short leave Burley was posted, as a raw recruit, to 32 Squadron, based at Biggin Hill in Kent. The unit have already been introduced in the chapter on John Flinders, and were a successful component of Fighter Command who had fought hard over France in the previous two months. They were soon to be in the thick of the action when the Battle of Britain commenced in July. Under the command of Sqn Ldr John 'Baron' Worrall (the 'Mandarin'), 32 boasted a number of veteran fighter pilots who had already cut their teeth on the Luftwaffe. The Bump suffered a series of heavy raids during the ensuing months, and the 32nd Pursuit also operated from the forward airfield at Hawkinge, patrolling over Channel convoys using the Straits of Dover, or 'Hell Fire Corner' as contemporary newspapers insisted on calling it. Burley had his first taste of action on 3 July, which was just a few days after he had joined the squadron. On that afternoon a handful of Dornier 17Z bombers of 8/KG77 launched a raid on the forward airfield at Manston on the North Foreland, achieving only minimal damage on this occasion. They then spread across south-east England, with some aircraft penetrating inland almost as far as London, aiming to attack the Kenley Sector airfield to the west of Biggin.

Higgins, piloting Hurricane N2670, was Blue 3 in 'B' Flight, accompanied by PO Peter Gardner and Sgt Edward Bayley. The trio intercepted one of the bombers at 4.45 p.m. after climbing through thick cloud extending to 15,000 feet. They chased the slim, twin-finned bandit through a mass of patchy cloud before Higgins' fighter broke into clear sky and closed for a stern attack. The rear gunner opened up as the Hurricane bored in, but an eight-second burst struck home and the Dornier lost height, dropping below cloud level. Higgins and Bayley pressed home further attacks, closing to within fifty yards and killing the rear gunner. Gardner also joined in the target practice against the hapless raider, all three fighters circling watchfully as the bomber, both engines knocked out, crash-landed in a large hopfield south-east of Paddock Wood at Baybrooks, near Horsmonden. Two crew members were killed in the combat, and the remains of the wrecked aeroplane, coded 3Z+GS, Wn 2642, were still visible ten years after the war. Burley had opened his Luftwaffe account with one-third of a Dornier very definitely confirmed.

The Squadron ORB shows that Higgins flew continuously on patrols and convoy escort during July and August, from both Biggin Hill and Hawkinge. He did not fire his guns again until 20 July when the squadron was scrambled in the late afternoon to defend a convoy with the interesting code name of 'Bosom', then under air attack 10 miles off Dover. Higgins flew as Green 3 to Sqn Ldr Worrall, as Green 1 and Sub-Lieutenant Geoffrey Bulmer, a Fleet Air Arm pilot on loan to the RAF, as Green 2. With two other squadrons in support, the 32nd waded into a whole *Geschwader* of Junkers 87B dive-bombers of 11/StG1, guarded by over fifty Messerschmitt 109s and 110s. Flying P3679, Higgins saw several twin-motor Me 110s below him at 9,000 feet, which he described as 'Jaguars' – a mythical bomber version of the escort fighter with a glazed nose. Slamming open his throttle, he pushed forward his control column and overtook one of the *Zerstörers*, which had just commenced a dive on an escorting destroyer. He opened fire at 300 yards and kept his firing button depressed for seven seconds, whilst around 1,000 rounds of .303 ammunition chased the two-seater, which began streaming smoke. Higgins broke away at 1,000 feet, seeing his victim continue his dive into the Channel, crashing in a great cloud of spray close by the destroyer and sinking almost instantaneously.

The rest of his section fared badly. Hit by 109s of 11/JG51, Bulmer was shot down into the sea. Worrall had his engine knocked out and force-landed near Hawkinge, vacating his cockpit just before his Hurricane went up in flames. Higgins was almost a third victim of the 109s. Gaining height after his victory over the 110, his fighter suddenly took hits from astern. Caught unawares, his first indication of the attack was when a hail of bullets drummed into his fuselage, hammering into the armour plate behind his seat. He was slightly wounded in the face by splinters, but was able to break sharply away from his attacker and lose him. His opponent was probably Hptm. Horst Tietzen, Staffelkapitan of 11/JG51. If so the Derbyshire pilot enjoyed a lucky escape, as Tietzen was at that time the fourth-highest-scoring Luftwaffe ace, with twenty tallies painted on his Messerschmitt's tailfin. Ironically, Tietzen himself went down a month later, killed off Whitstable on 18 August.

32 Squadron continued to fly daily sorties from their home base and Hawkinge throughout late July and early August, although Burley saw no action until the 12th of the latter month, when a late-afternoon patrol intercepted around thirty aircraft identified as 'Dornier 215s', escorted by twenty to thirty Me 109s. The Hurricanes met the enemy formation at 5.15 p.m., 12,000 feet above Dover. The squadron tangled with the 109s and became enmeshed in a furious dogfight over the coast. In this sort of close-quarter mêlée, the Hurricanes, with their superior manoeuvrability, held the advantage. Higgins, piloting N2524, fastened on to the tail of an enemy fighter, who was unable to shake him off. He fired a series of bursts, closing from 300 to 100 yards, seeing his tracer strike home as the 109, trailing smoke, fell away towards the sea in a flat spin. With its pilot obviously dead, the Messerschmitt hit the water off Manston, its demise marked only by a spreading circle of foam. Burley climbed back to the still-continuing battle. Seeing a second Me 109 below, he turned to attack but his opponent, having caught sight of the Hurricane, dived away to sea level. Burley opened fire at 300 yards, but the faster German gradually drew away from his straining warplane as, throttle through the gate, he pursued it across the Channel. Realising he could not close the range, a frustrated Higgins broke away and returned home.

By the middle of August the tired survivors of the 32nd Pursuit, many of whom had been flying and fighting almost non-stop since Dunkirk, had just about reached their limit. The crisis was exacerbated by the second phase of the Luftwaffe's battle tactics, which concentrated on the Kentish fighter airfields of 11 Group, subjecting the weary pilots to increasing pressures in the air

Left: *Burley as an uncertified teacher at his old school, Whitwell Senior, in 1933.* (M. Hopkins)
Right: *William Burley Higgins in 1939, just before the outbreak of war.* (N. Fryer)

'D' Flight, 5 SFTS, Sealand, in spring 1940, showing the first intake to train on the new Miles Master I. Burley is middle row, second left, with Ray Holmes on his left, and 'Wag' Haw is third left in the top row. Ray Holmes helped shoot down the Dornier 17Z which fell on Victoria Station on 15 September 1940. (R. Holmes)

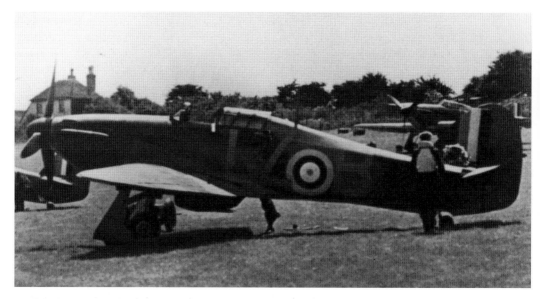

Hurricane Is of 32 Squadron prepare for take-off from their forward base at Hawkinge during the Battle. P3144 GZ-B is in the foreground, with GZ-T on the left.

This 8/KG77 Dornier 17Z (3Z+GS), fuselage pocked with bullet-strikes from Higgins' Blue Section Hurricanes, slid into a Kentish hopfield at Baybrooks, Horsmonden, on 3 July 1940. (Kent Messenger)

and on the ground. 32 Squadron struggled on until almost the end of the month, with their tiredness reflected in mounting losses. Burley's final combat with the unit took place on 24 August. Their Hurricanes flew a number of patrols on this date, culminating in a teatime scramble when five aircraft of 'A' Flight, prowling over Hawkinge, were vectored on to bandits near Folkestone. At 4 p.m. the Hurricanes ran into around fifteen 109s at 10,000 feet, and a general dogfight ensued. Burley, again flying P3679, closed with one of the square-winged, shark-like enemy fighters. At 300 yards he managed to pull round on his opponent's tail, hanging on like grim death and expending all 2,800 rounds in his ammunition bays. In his combat report, he described how his antagonist was struck continuously by a series of brief bursts as he shortened the range from 300 to under 100 yards. The enemy pilot was by this time almost certainly dead, as he made no effort to avoid the tracer from Higgins' machine guns, finally nosing over into a gentle dive and plunging into the Channel 10 miles off Folkestone. The Me 109 disappeared in a plume of spray, taking its pilot down to the distant sea bed. As Burley commented in his combat report: 'I did not see the pilot bale out and saw no movement where the A/C sank.' This success brought Higgins' tally to three and one shared victories, all dutifully painted on the improvised squadron scoreboard – the wingtip from a Hurricane – which can today be seen in the Battle of Britain Museum at Hendon.

Three days later the survivors of the bloody but unbowed unit received orders to prepare to move out for rest and recuperation, and on 28 August they flew north to Acklington after their relief squadron, No.79, had arrived to replace them. Higgins, a veteran after almost two months' hard fighting, was granted some well-deserved leave. He had been engaged to Dorothy Fryer from Worksop for some time, and her younger brother Norman remembered Burley sleeping solidly for 36 hours after his return home! Norman also recalled how tense and highly-strung the fighter pilot seemed, although Burley always had the feeling he would never be killed in action. He revealed to the agog young Norman how formidable a fighting machine the Messerschmitt 109 was, and how deadly and calculating a game aerial combat could be; a far cry from the casual, chivalrous image portrayed in the popular press.

Burley looked forward to the time when Fighter Command could take the battle over to the Continent and meet the Germans on their side of the English Channel. Norman Fryer's overriding impressions of his future brother-in-law at this time were of a taut, keyed-up – though fearless – professional, willing to take his chance and eager to get to grips with the enemy again. This eagerness led Burley to respond to a call for volunteers to return south to the battle. On 9 September he was posted to 253 Squadron, which was another Hurricane unit based at Kenley. 253 had joined the conflict on 29 August after a spell at Prestwick in Scotland.

During the Battle of Britain, and indeed the entire war, there were good, bad and indifferent fighter squadrons in the RAF, as in the air forces of all the combatant nations. The merit of a squadron often lay in the leadership potential of its squadron and flight commanders; a swift turnover among leaders often had an unsettling effect on the pilots concerned. 609 were forged from an average into a first-rate unit by Sqn Ldr Darley, and the squadron's flight leaders were also of a high calibre. There were also lucky and unlucky squadrons; 609 were both well led and lucky. By contrast, 253 were markedly unlucky when they were thrown into the ring. Between 30 August and 15 September, the unit lost ten Hurricanes, with seven pilots killed in action. Two of these seem to have been deliberately machine-gunned by 109s when descending by parachute.

On 253's first day in action, which was the 30th, four Hurricanes were shot down with three pilots killed, while a further Hurricane force-landed and three others suffered varied combat damage. On the following morning, Sqn Ldr Harold Starr, the CO, was killed. Later that day Tom Gleave, his replacement, who had dispatched four Me 109s the previous day in a few minutes' furious action, attacked a Junkers 88 and baled out of his Hurricane very badly burned. A third squadron aircraft crash-landed. These dispiriting losses in aircraft and personnel mounted almost daily through early September, to say nothing of the fliers who, like Gleave, were wounded.

Fresh pilots were drafted into the unit, including Burley, who flew his first sortie with the badly-mauled squadron on 11 September. On that day he piloted Hurricane R2686 as Yellow 2 in 'A' Flight. The formation intercepted a considerable number of enemy aircraft, identified as Dornier 215s, but more likely to have been bomb-carrying Messerschmitt 110s, over Maidstone at 3.45 p.m. at 16,000 feet. The raiders, flying in sections echelon starboard and escorted by 109s and 110s above, were heading for London and were picked out by anti-aircraft fire speckling the air around them.

The squadron bored in to attack, firing and breaking away at close range before pulling round for further assaults. During these concentrated and fast-moving clashes, several German bombers fell away from the formation trailing smoke and flames, but it was impossible to check on individual results. Some pilots saw at least half-a-dozen parachutes drifting down in the wake of the stricken swarm, one of them on fire. Burley's aeroplane was hit several times by concentrated return fire, but none of the strikes was serious. Following one attack, he found himself challenged by a lone Me 109. After some initial manoeuvrings, he glued his Hurricane on to the enemy fighter's tail, and a point-blank burst from his eight Brownings set it on fire over Newhaven. The 109E-4, Wn 1641, from 2/JG51, crashed in flames at Houndean Bottom, carrying its pilot Hptm. Wiggers, Staffelkapitan and an Experte of the unit, to his death.

During 1978 the Wealden Aviation Archaeological Group investigated the crash site not far from the A27 and the Lewes to Brighton railway line. A resident presented them with a swastika-emblazoned fin panel purloined from the wreck thirty-eight years before.

Momentarily circling Wiggers' billowing funeral pyre, Higgins then flew back across Kent to the Thames Estuary. He came up behind a dozen 110s, manoeuvring to get in a two-second burst at the rearmost. Clouds of white smoke began streaming from the rear of the escort fighter. At that moment several 109s intervened and, low on fuel and ammunition, Burley broke off the engagement and returned to base.

Burley fought his last battle over the Isle of Sheppey on the afternoon of 14 September. At around 3.20 p.m. that day, seven Hurricanes from 253 took off to patrol Tenterden, with Higgins piloting P5184. The formation consisted of two vics of three, with a seventh fighter to the rear. The local Controller vectored them towards Maidstone to intercept a raid coming in at 15,000 feet. When they were 5 miles west of Faversham, the Hurricanes turned south-west into the sun and were hit by a shoal of yellow-nosed 109s from JG26 over Sheppey. Little is known of Burley's last combat, but P5184 was seen from the ground, losing height and apparently out of control. One other aircraft of 253 was shot down, but its wounded pilot baled out over Faversham. On the credit side, an Me 109 blew up under fire during the mêlée, killing the pilot.

Seeing Higgins' Hurricane come down 3 miles from him, John Kirkpatrick of Sittingbourne, who had watched the whirling action above him, drove to the scene at Swanton Farm, Bredgar, and dragged the young pilot's body from the cockpit. Among Burley's belongings he found a letter from his fiancée, with her address but signed only 'Dorothy'. The next day he wrote her a letter, which deserves quoting in full:

17 Newlands Avenue,
Sittingbourne, Kent.
15.9.40

Dear Miss Dorothy,

I trust you will forgive me writing this letter to you but I feel you may like to know of the wonderful battle I saw on Saturday afternoon when a German fighter was brought down by Sergeant Higgins who was flying a Hurricane fighter. It was a severe fight and it appeared to me that your dear brave friend was not satisfied in getting only one of them but went in for a second time. His plane had

Under the gaze of interested spectators, an airman inspects the spread-eagle insignia of KG77 under the cockpit of the wrecked Dornier. A coloured three-view illustration of this aircraft appears in F.K. Mason's Battle over Britain, *albeit with an incorrect date of destruction.* (Kent Messenger)

Hurricane P3522 GZ-V runs up its Merlin in readiness for a scramble from Hawkinge, one of the nearest bases to occupied France.

been hit and he may not have known this fact. Then he came down, hunted for a landing ground (and he must have been very badly wounded) because he was unable to land the plane and I am sorry to tell you that he was in my opinion killed before he reached the ground. I pulled his body from the plane, which was on fire, and found a letter, the only one, apparently written by you with only your Christian name as signature. I only took your address and name and handed the rest of his belongings to the police. If you have not had official word of this tragedy I trust you will not take exception to my writing.

I offer my deepest sympathy and know you will agree when I say he died a gallant death to save us all. We have had continuous air fights all day today. His plane clock stopped at exactly four o'clock Saturday afternoon. The personal belongings consisted of one Ingersoll watch, six one-pound notes, one ten-shilling note and half-a-crown. His fountain pen was broken to pieces and pocket wallet destroyed. He died at Bredgar, Kent 3 miles from where I live. I jumped in my car and made towards the scene while his plane was still in the air. My wife asks me to express her sorrow to you. She saw him bring the German crashing to earth.

Yours sincerely,
J. Kirkpatrick.

It is interesting to note that the Kirkpatricks confirmed the destruction of an enemy aeroplane to Burley, though this last kill must be forever conjectural. The young pilot died, ironically, on the

Hptm. Horst Tietzen was an Experte of JG51, and may have met Burley in combat near Dover on 27 July 1940, when the Derbyshire pilot's Hurricane was hit by fire from an Me 109.

114

The funeral pyre of Hptm. Ernst Wiggers' Me 109E of JG51, which was shot down by Burley on 11 September 1940 and blazed in a field at Houndean Bottom, just above the A27 Brighton Road near Lewes. Note the halted traffic, presumably viewing the remains of the burning fighter.
(Saunders Collection)

eve of Sunday 15 September: the day before Fighter Command's most telling victory, when it repulsed and decimated successive armadas of Goering's bombers. He was only thirteen days short of his 27th birthday.

With at least four and one shared combat victories to his credit, Higgins had achieved the status of an ace, and it is notable that apart from the shared Dornier, his four kills were all German fighters – a Messerschmitt 110 and three of the potent Me 109s – which, on paper at least, outclassed his slower Hurricane on most counts. Burley's abilities were well appreciated by his comrades-in-arms, and Norman Fryer believes that at the time of his death he was in line for both a medal and a commission. Regrettably, neither came to pass.

The news of the death of their local hero cast a deep gloom over Whitwell, where his exploits had been well publicised. The local children especially venerated him as their ex-teacher and as an RAF stalwart, and one of a glamorous breed whose exploits were making daily front-page news. His body was brought home to Derbyshire and borne to St Lawrence's Church by army lorry, followed by a lengthy procession which included a host of representatives from local military and civilian associations. Blinds were drawn throughout the neighbourhood and flags flew at half-mast. Hundreds lined the pavements to pay their last respects as the cortège passed by. The churchyard was crowded and the church packed to capacity with mourners, including his fiancée, Dorothy, and children who had gathered to give their popular schoolmaster a last farewell. No more would they wave to Burley on autumn Saturday mornings as he motorcycled along the north Derbyshire

The 32 Squadron scoreboard, painted on the wingtip of a Hawker Hurricane and now displayed at the Battle of Britain Museum, Hendon. The combat victories of John Flinders and Burley Higgins are recorded here. (Author)

lanes, gun across his shoulders, with his springer spaniel invariably perched on top of the petrol tank. This cheery, determined, exceptional man was now but a fond memory.

Burley Higgins was laid in his native earth in a quiet corner of Whitwell churchyard. His brother, Edward Michael – another RAF pilot, who flew Dakotas in Burma and during the Berlin Airlift – is buried in the same plot. He died in 1961 when his Derby Airways DC-3 crashed in the Pyrenees, near Perpignan. A third brother, James Stewart, was another RAF pilot, who flew obsolescent Battle light bombers in France, attacking Wehrmacht columns in the spring of 1940: one sure way of not achieving longevity at the time. However, he did survive, duly attaining the rank of wing commander and being decorated with the Distinguished Flying Cross.

One ironic postscript was the bizarre death of Burley's ex-fiancée. Dorothy Fryer joined the ATS, and one evening in 1942 she was celebrating her first leave with friends in Worksop. In the blackout their car crashed into an army tank, whose crew had left it parked without lights. The other passengers escaped with minor injuries, but Dorothy was tragically killed. She died only two years after her courageous fiancé, one of a brave band of brothers, fell whilst defending the skies over his homeland.

eight

Squadron Leader
Norman Vipan Glew

Combat Record

Date	Sqn	Locality	Aircraft Flown	Enemy Type	Claim
02.09.40	72	Dungeness	Spitfire I P9460	Messerschmitt 110C	Destroyed
				Messerschmitt 109E	Probable
07.09.40	72	Maidstone/Dartford	Spitfire I K9841	Dornier 17Z	Damaged
				Dornier 17Z	Damaged
				Dornier 17Z	Damaged
10.09.40	72	Weybridge	Spitfire I P9376	Dornier 17Z	Destroyed (shared)
				Dornier 17Z	Destroyed (shared)
23.09.40	72	Folkestone	Spitfire I R6881	Messerschmitt 109E	Destroyed (shared)
24.09.40	72	Rochester	Spitfire I R6881	Junkers 88A	Probable
27.09.40	72	Dungeness	Spitfire I X4881 RN-M	Messerschmitt 110D	Destroyed
				Messerschmitt 109E	Damaged
12.10.40	72	Dungeness	Spitfire I X4252	Messerschmitt 109E	Damaged
04.07.41	260	Talia	Hurricane I	LeO 451	Damaged (ground)
09.07.41	260	Aleppo	Hurricane I	LeO 257bis	Destroyed (ground)
				Potez 63	Damaged (ground)
02.01.42	260	Agedabia	Hurricane I	Messerschmitt 109F	Damaged
18.01.42	260	Benghazi	Hurricane I	Junkers 87B	Destroyed
02.04.42	260	N.W. Tobruk	Kittyhawk II	Messerschmitt 109F	Damaged

Squadron Leader Norman Vipan Glew

I KNOW as much or more about Norman Glew – 'Boy' to his family and (inevitably) 'Sticky' to his friends – as of any pilot whose deeds are recorded in this book. Two of his sisters are still living, and several Service colleagues who flew alongside him have contributed recollections of him. Unfortunately his logbooks are no longer extant, but to some extent they are compensated for by surviving combat reports, diaries which he kept fitfully, and a number of letters. Sticky was 'a strong character, both on the ground and in the air'. He was a forthright, popular and uncomplicated personality, who was so proud of his mother's family that he joined her maiden name, Vipan, to his own, although he never made the addition official.

Norman Glew was born in Derby in November 1916 to Captain Norman and Mildred Glew, who also had three daughters. His father served with the Sherwood Foresters in the First World War, and worked as an auditor for the London, Midland & Scottish Railway. During the Second World War he was Adjutant to the 9th Battalion of the local Home Guard. 'Boy' attended Bemrose School alongside other Derbeians who were to serve with distinction in RAF Fighter Command, such as Alan Feary, Frank Walker-Smith and John van Schaick. From an early age Norman was an aviation enthusiast, and his sisters remember that his books and bedroom walls were covered with drawings, sketches and photographs of aircraft. His sole ambition was to become a pilot, but his father opposed a career move to that end, and the frustrated son had to endure training as a dispensing chemist at Boots before he was able to join the local RAFVR in November 1938 at the age of nineteen.

Up until the outbreak of war, Norman notched up over 100 flying hours in Magisters, Hart variants and Tiger Moths at No.11 E&RFTS at Prestwick, a course he shared with Norman Taylor and other local VRs. Sticky's diaries for 1940 and part of 1941 have been preserved, and their comments and snippets are vital for an understanding of what made this young man tick. His younger sister, Pauline, described him as 'a devil-may-care, happy-go-lucky sort of chap who had no time for pettiness, hypocrisy and bigotry'. On the rare occasions he took her to school, he deliberately motored straight up the drive, knowing it was officially out of bounds, just to cock a snook at authority. His diaries show a keen, spirited, press-on type, anxious to complete his training and get into the war, and no stranger to the attractions of drink and the opposite sex. The names of sundry young ladies flit across the pages, including that of his special girlfriend, Jean Offiler, a relation of the family behind the Derby brewing firm. He had sound sense to pick a lady with the right connections!

When war broke out Glew was mobilised, but then waited impatiently until his posting to No.1 ITW at Cambridge in early November. His course were billeted at Emmanuel College, and were drilled and lectured until Christmas when they impatiently awaited their postings to Flying Training Schools. This is reflected in his jottings which bring out the boredom, sharpened by the lack of flying, though relieved by numerous pub crawls, assignations with lady friends, and the frequent skipping of parades. The contemporary term for inebriation was 'whistled' and the word occurs frequently. Despite his addiction to the hop, he wrote in January 1940: 'Drink taken sparingly is OK, but real booze-ups only give pleasure for a few hours, otherwise they are hellish.' Since he wrote at the same time 'women are mere ornaments', his state of mind could perhaps be appreciated and excused, except perhaps by feminists and the Temperance Movement!

A weekend in Brighton with Derby colleagues Tony Evershed and Ted Hives helped dispel the gloom, but heavy snow and mists enhanced the Cambridge depression, which only eased when the course were finally drafted to No.3 FTS at South Cerney, Gloucestershire. Glew was so determined to get there, he swore he would escape 'if it means crawling out on hands and knees'. Things did improve once he settled in at South Cerney. 'We've started our war career in earnest', he wrote, 'we're all set'. Other Derby VR friends were in similar situations nearby – Feary, Hunt, Wardel-Knight and others – and they often dropped in for a night or two on the town. On leave in February he met Jean, and but for the war would doubtless have become engaged. 'She's looking more attractive than ever', he

Squadron Leader Norman Vipan Glew RAFVR is in the cockpit of a Spitfire Mk V in 1943. Note the crowbar clipped to the inside of the cockpit door. (P. Sturdy)

Norman is standing in the centre back row in this group photograph of the trainees at No.11 E&RFTS, Prestwick, Ayr, March 1939. (J. Jackson)

confided to his diary, 'I like her more each leave'. However, he was determined to avoid all serious attachments whilst the war lasted and the pair did not marry. Following his posting abroad in May 1941, he never saw her again.

On 10 February, after five months, Norman was in the air again, flying a Hart biplane. Off-duty, it was a round of imbibing, dances, the odd show and plenty of female company. 'I'm all for these WAAFs', he wrote, 'they're damn good sports and work hard for their country'. In the early days of the war there was often open friction between the VRs and the Regular Air Force. Many of the latter felt that flying was a quick and easy way to three stripes, and Norman reported, 'the VRs aren't going down too well with the regulars. Well, the airmen can go to hell. Any troublemaking will come from their side, not ours'. PT, and the occasional outdoor team game helped to sweat the alcohol out of the fledgling pilots' systems, along with the cold and windy flying conditions which buffeted the fragile Hinds. 'Bounced to buggery', was one of his comments after a bumpy session. At ground shooting with the Vickers machine gun, he gained nearly full marks. As the weather improved their aircraft began ranging further – on solos, map exercises and formation flights – and he struggled hard 'to get polish' to his flying. 'The idea is to fly well without effort', he confided. By late March, he felt this polish was coming. He thought the Hind was not modern enough for their purposes, and wished for Harvards or Masters. Hangovers continued, particularly on hectic weekends to London and meetings with former colleagues of the Derby VR.

Night flying was added to the schedule in April, plus cross-country exercises and the occasional trip in twin-motor trainers. Sticky developed an aversion to the Airspeed Oxfords they sometimes used. 'Don't like 'em', he confessed, 'very heavy, swishing about the sky'. Two of his aerial pastimes involved low flying – 'beat-ups' and aerobatics – and in the run-up to his wings examination, he indulged in both. Despite his intensive study of theory and ground subjects, there was time for beer-hazed off-duty bouts and assignations. With a gang of companions he went to the England-Wales rugby match at Gloucester on the 13th. Afterwards there was time for tea and a booze-up. 'Everyone happy', he declared later, 'some danced, some grabbed women. I stuck to beer.' He purchased a car on 20 April and finished the course a day later, completing 59 flying hours – a grand total of 170 all told.

After a short leave, when he skilfully juggled two girlfriends (Jean and Joy) around, advanced training began. He enjoyed this, remarking: 'one is treated more as a pilot than a school child. More responsibility is given to one.' A lively weekend in London followed in early May, with two nights at the Cumberland, leg shows and a 'terrific party' at the Café Anglais where he met the bandleader Harry Roy. There was a subsequent period of concentrated flying with practice attacks, practice bombing, cross-countries and aerobatics, all imbued with a sense of urgency as Germany launched her *Blitzkrieg* on the West. The pressure eased off in June, with some time for relaxation in the hot weather, as the young aviators impatiently awaited postings from the school. His last flight with the unit was on the 14th, when he celebrated his departure with a virtuoso performance when he 'turned the plane inside out. Upward flick rolls &c.' He read his confidential report, which was a glowing one, praising him as a 'sound air pilot. Very smooth and determined.'

After a final leave in Derby, the serious work began. On 18 June, Norman was posted to 72 Spitfire Squadron based at Acklington. Here, many of his compatriots from No.3 FTS were gathered – Sergeants Johnny White, Bill Rolls, Johnny Gilders and PO Ernest Males. He joined 'A' Flight and began practice sessions to prepare himself for flying the Spitfire. These involved a few hours on Magisters, followed by a couple of outings on a Harvard, learning to adjust to a retractable undercarriage, flaps and a variable-pitch airscrew. On the 25th he finally got his hands on the sleek Supermarine monoplane, loving the lively and elegant fighter from the outset. 'Like them immensely', he wrote, 'beautiful machine'. PO Jimmy Elsdon was given the task of teaching the five ex-3 FTS greenhorns how to fly and fight this finest of interceptors. A few months earlier Elsdon had flown alongside Lawrie Henstock from Ashbourne in a section attack on a flight of Heinkel IIIs, which sent two of the German raiders crashing into the North Sea.

Elsdon worked the five hard in a whole series of combat manoeuvres – formation flights, attacks and drogue firing, battle climbs, peel-offs and dives. On 8 July, 152 Squadron, who shared the airfield with 72, were shifted south to Warmwell on the Dorset coast. 'Lucky dogs', wrote Norman. With them went PO Douglas Shepley from Holmesfield, who, one month later, plunged to a watery grave somewhere off the Needles. 152 were replaced by 79 Squadron, which Glew somewhat tartly and unfairly described as 'a dead beat crew'. On the 23rd he heard of the death in combat of the second of the Derby VRs, his old friend Tony Evershed, shot down on 9 July while flying Spitfires with 54 Squadron.

At the beginning of August, Elsdon was satisfied that the 'five sprogs' were fit to take their place in the squadron's operational line-up. They had gained their appellation via 72's officers, who, according to Bill Rolls, were good types, friendly and approachable. When the five came down to flights, the old hands invariably referred to them as 'sprogs' and in the bar one night they decided to paint the designation on the backs of their Mae Wests, together with an appropriate number. Sticky was 'Sprog 5'. It provided a good laugh, and the officers concerned considered the gesture a very sporting one, gaining their respect. The quintet bought a silver-plated tankard inscribed 'From the Five Sprogs. For Patience and Devotion to Duty', and presented it to a pleased and surprised Jimmy Elsdon.

In August 1940, 72 were ordered to operate their Spitfires by night, which was not a popular decree as the sensitive fighter, with its long nose and narrow undercarriage, was among the least successful nominations for a role it was never designed for. There were some hairy incidents involving the 'sprogs'. Gilders turned his aircraft over one night, and White and Rolls taxied into unseen obstacles in the darkness. Norman had a nasty pile-up himself, hitting the ground a hundred yards on the wrong side of the airfield. His machine burst into flames, but he scrambled out unhurt. On the 30th he began six days' leave, borrowing the squadron Magister to fly to Burnaston with a colleague who stayed the night. The next day brought an urgent telegram with a dreaded summons: 72 were moving south to join in the action, and Norman's presence was requested. He flew back solo to Acklington, only to find his unit had moved to Biggin Hill.

Sticky drove hard down to his new base, only to discover that because of the heavy damage inflicted on the airfield and its buildings, his squadron had been temporarily diverted to Croydon. He climbed into a Spitfire and landed there on the evening of the 31 August. 72 had already been in action and had suffered casualties. 'What a bloody life in store for us', was his immediate thought, as he steeled himself for the task he had been preparing for since he joined the VR nearly two years before. The NCO pilots' billets at Croydon were anything but comfortable; in fact, little more than a disgrace. So depressing and inadequate were they that the CO, Sqn Ldr 'Ted' Graham, had to intervene to shift them to better quarters.

Norman Glew went into action for the first time at half-past seven on the morning of 2 September, piloting Spitfire P9460. This was the celebrated 'Sergeants' Scramble'; the NCO pilots, billeted in tents close by dispersal, heard the warning and roared off to intercept an incoming raid. Lounging in their mess, the officers missed out and were mightily peeved to have been left behind. The sergeants met a formation of bombers screened by Me 109s over the Thames Estuary. Norman found himself behind a Messerschmitt, and coolant vapour was soon streaming from its radiators in a thin mist as he fired his eight Brownings from astern. It fell away, but he was too wise to follow it down with other predatory companions lurking above. He later claimed a probable, landing at Rochester to refuel. Later in the day he flew down to Hawkinge for two further patrols. In the first of these he sent down a Messerschmitt 110 escort, which fell into the Channel off Dungeness, and which was confirmed as destroyed three days later. Several *Zerstörers* of ZG26 perished in action on this day, and one of these was probably Norman's prey. After this combat he landed, lost, at West Malling. 'What a day of warfare!' he wrote later of his initial kill: 'My first confirmed victory. Wonder how many more before I bite it?'

Glew was given 24 hours' leave on 3 September and managed 3 hours at home! For some days he could not add to his tally, seeing many Huns but having little luck. On the 7th he wrote: 'This bloody

Left: *Uffz. Dilthey's crippled Me 109 scrapes over the Folkestone Mole, undercarriage dangling, before flopping into the harbour. Above, Norman's Spitfire symbolically overflies his victim.* (Cornwell Collection)
Right: *The 'five sprogs', 72 Squadron, Acklington, Summer 1940. From left to right, back row: Sgt J. Gilders, PO E. Males, Sgt W.T. Rolls. Front row: Sgt J. White, Sgt N.V. Glew.* (W.T. Rolls)

Sergeant Glew (on the right) chats with his flight commander and the squadron intelligence officer, 41 Squadron, Catterick, April 1941. (P. Sturdy)

Long-range Hurricane 1s of 260 Squadron ranged on the deck of HMS Ark Royal before flying off to Malta, 14 June 1941. Note the fixed under wing fuel tanks in position. (P. Sturdy)

Between Gibraltar and Malta Norman took this shot of aircraft of his unit and the escorting Lockheed Hudson VX-K of 206 Squadron. (P. Sturdy)

pace is hot. The Squadron won't stand it for long. We wrote-off thirty Spits in the first week. Replacements coming in right and left.' That afternoon, in action over the Maidstone-Dartford locality around 5.30 p.m. in K9841, which was a clapped-out remount handed over by 616 Squadron, he attacked a force of Dornier 17s in company with three other Spitfires of 72, spraying a trio of them with incendiary rounds, seeing the tracers going into the enemy warplanes in a five-second burst, before Me 110s approaching from astern forced a break away. He then intercepted a 110, but pulled away to drive another escort fighter off PO Norfolk's tail. A claim of three Dornier 17s damaged was allowed.

In the late afternoon of the 10th, piloting P9376, Norman and four other squadron members reported two 'Dornier 215s' shot down between Weybridge and East Grinstead, presumably claiming a fifth-share in each kill. One of these was a 17Z-3 of 9/KG76, coded F1+ET Wn 2778, which crashed at West Hoathley with two dead crewmen aboard. By this time Norman's nerves were causing a temporary nausea and he was unable to eat. However, he did not have much chance for food, as there were just 'too many flaps'. Croydon was 'deadbeat', as the NCOs had been moved into houses adjoining the airfield. The buildings lacked electricity, water and, in fact, any creature comforts which made life bearable. Their duty began at 5.30 a.m., and ended at 10 p.m. 'Every day the same', he wrote, though the unit operated a 24 hours on, 24 hours off routine at the time. 'About four scraps a day take place here', he informed his parents. 'This scrapping makes one damn tired and the more sleep the better.'

On 12 September, 72 Squadron gratefully moved back to the Bump, where the food and living conditions were a great improvement on Croydon. The five NCO sprogs, swiftly becoming battle-hardened veterans, roomed and imbibed together. The late Bill Rolls got to know Sticky well at this time, though Johnny Gilders was Norman's closest friend. 'He was popular with everyone in the squadron', Bill wrote in a letter to me:

> … and was well known for his moustache and pipe. He was honest in making his opinions known … I was always pleased to see when we were on the same sortie; he was a determined flier who, I am sure, shot down more aircraft than he claimed for. He did not like the paperwork involved.

Bill claimed that Sticky's forceful manner was worth many free pints in various hostelries. He would 'chat up the people nearby as though he had known them for ages' and, in the thick of the Battle of Britain, nothing was too good for the men of the RAF Fighter Command. Norman wrote on the 18th: 'Had a few odd beers – never have to buy them ourselves though – civvies very good.'

The sprogs remained in the midst of the hectic action; both Males and White had to bale out, and Gilders once staggered home with a hard-hit aeroplane. On one occasion some of the sprogs set out to find Johnny White when he force-landed near London docks. He was eventually run to earth in a local pub, 'tight as a newt and shooting a colossal line'. When the pilots got him into their car they found his pockets stuffed with coins and currency notes, pushed there by a grateful populace! On 15 September, Jimmy Elsdon was shot down, and with an incendiary leg wound was out of action for the remainder of the Battle. Norman himself had settled down by this time; he was sleeping better and his appetite had improved. 'Enjoying it, more or less', was the cryptic comment in his diary.

On the 17th he boasted of graduating to his own personal Spitfire, which he named 'Emma', probably after a tough and warm-hearted East End lady they had met during White's dockland adventure. The plane was coded RN-M, and on both sides of the cockpit coaming he painted his emblem – a large red circle enclosing an angular question mark. Alongside were two small swastikas, presumably indicating his one and one shared victories. 'My Spit is grand', he confided, 'smooth engine and trimmed beautifully. The crew are grand too. These boys work hard and get little thanks.' On the 21st, recently commissioned PO Norfolk incurred his displeasure by diving 'N' too fast and distorting the wings. The machine was consigned to the AST fighter repair unit at Hamble for realignment, and it is probable that Norman told his colleague exactly what he thought of him.

On 23 September, Norman scored another combat victory. He was flying R6881 on a patrol over Gravesend at around ten in the morning as Green 2, when his formation was attacked by Me 109s. Climbing away from the attack, he saw two further single-seaters from JG2 heading south, and dived on the rearmost yellow-nose, hitting it with a four-second burst from 250 yards. The Messerschmitt half-rolled into a steep dive, with its undercarriage dangling in the slipstream. The accompanying 109 swung to attack, but Glew turned sharply onto its tail, squeezing his gun button for two seconds as his quarry pulled across his sights and rapidly disappeared. The Derbyshire pilot lost height in an effort to locate his original target, seeing it way below, under fire from PO Ivor Cosby, flying as Blue 3. Glew joined in the target practice, and their combined fire settled the German fighter's fate. With its undercarriage dangling like the legs of a wounded bird and the pilot wounded in the shoulder, the Messerschmitt stuttered over Folkestone Harbour, narrowly avoiding a terminal collision with the Mole. The crippled yellow-nosed 109E-4, piloted by Uffz. Dilthey of 4/JG2 flopped into the sea, raising a colossal cloud of spray. When it subsided, the tail unit was the only visible marker of Wn 1969, coded 2+-.

Dilthey, who broke his leg in the ditching, was a lucky man. Lieutenant M.E. Jacobs and Lance-Corporal Len Ebbington of the Royal Engineers stripped off their jackets and dived into the water to help him into a fishing boat, as a victorious Spitfire performed a series of overhead rolls to the delight of the watchers on shore. Unknown to Norman, a *Daily Mirror* photographer had set up his long-distance lens on the cliff-top in the expectation of some action in this war-torn part of Kent. He was not disappointed, and the next morning a million homes saw the dramatic photographs splashed across the front page, with captions describing the whole episode, and Sticky's Spitfire symbolically overflying his vanquished foe. He sent an annotated cutting to his family, scribbling in the justified line-shoot: 'Whoopee – wheel 'em in! All my own work!'

Squadron Leader 'Dickie' Mount's Hurricane, coded '1', on the way to Malta. (P. Sturdy)

On the morning of 24 September, 72 met 'a bunch of fifty-plus Huns escorted by fighters. Real mix-up.' The enemy were flying north-west over the Thames Estuary in the Rochester area at 8.45 a.m. and Norman, operating as Yellow 4, followed his comrades in line-astern into the mêlée. He closed on a Junkers 88 from below and behind, and at 250 yards saw his tracers converging on the starboard engine. Strikes sparkled across the nacelle, which began to drag a thickening scarf of oily black smoke before bursting into flames. The raider fell away in a left-hand spiral, and was immediately savaged by further Spitfires, who tore into it like predatory birds. Norman throttled away into a climb, pulling towards a covey of Me 109s above him. He aimed a burst at one before turning for base. In his combat report, in which he claimed a probable Ju 88, he noted that his magazines contained more incendiary rounds than the usual allotment, and believed this increased the effectiveness of his fire against the bandit's motor. It is unfortunately not known whether he himself had requested the extra incendiary mix, or if it was added as a general squadron experiment. On the 25th he got his hands on a brand-new Spitfire, X4481, only recently delivered and, like his previous one, coded RN-M. 'She's mine', he exulted, 'I picked up a good one which the flight commander had missed.'

The 27th brought Norman another success. The squadron, following 92, intercepted an escorted raid at 18,000 feet over Sevenoaks in mid-morning. He chased a formation, which he identified as Dornier 17s, but which were perhaps Messerschmitt 110s, as the two types were often mistaken for each other during the Battle. Flying as Yellow 3, he aimed a two-second burst at a 'Dornier 215' and saw the twin-finned empennage break away from the fuselage as both engines gushed flame. Glew surmised that other Spitfires had also fired at this target, as he dived to starboard and selected a 'Dornier 17' which was most likely a Messerschmitt 110 fighter-bomber, probably from ZG26. There are some puzzling factors concerning this engagement; notably that the raider was reported as carrying a crew of at least three, and that it jettisoned a stick of five bombs when under attack. He lined up the twin-engined,

Norman and his ground crew in front of Hurricane 'E' on an airstrip in Palestine in June 1941. The picture is captioned 'A unit of the Middle-East Air Force'. (P. Sturdy)

Above: *Norman poses in the cockpit of his Hurricane I sometime during the summer of 1941.* (J. Jackson)

Above right: *Through the gunsight. A pilot's eye view of the cockpit of Glew's Hurricane, showing the Barr and Stroud GM2 reflector gunsight.* (J. Jackson)

Below right: *A tropicalised Hurricane I of 260 Squadron, wheels and flaps down, comes in to land at El Bassa, Palestine, in August 1941. Norman described the airstrip as being 'at the base of a damn great hill'.* (J. Jackson)

twin-finned target in his GM2 reflector, putting in a four-second burst which stopped the port motor dead. Two other Spitfires came sniffing up, but pulled away on seeing that Norman 'was the rightful owner'. A second burst killed the rear gunner, whose fire suddenly ceased. Shovelling out black smoke, the enemy warplane fell away and headed for the deck, with Norman thumbing tracer in a series of quarter attacks, until the clatter of empty breech blocks told him he was out of ammunition.

By the time hunter and hunted had reached the coast near Dungeness, the German was almost at ground level, pulling violently up at the last moment to avoid a line of pylons ahead. In sheer frustration, Sticky aimed X4481 in a steep power-dive in an attempt to force his adversary down. The enemy pilot, presumably panicking as the Spitfire screamed past him with inches to spare, belly-landed into the Channel off Dungeness at around 10 a.m., leaving a long trail of oil in the sea behind him. Glew saw the crew scramble from the half-submerged wreckage and slip into the water. He amused himself by diving on the wallowing men, obliging them to duck underwater, fearful he was about to strafe them. He then directed a fishing trawler to the scene, which picked up the survivors. 'Had fun diving on the bastards while they were in the water', he wrote later, 'I bet they were full of seawater, the blighters.' The only contender for Glew's victim was a Messerschmitt 110D-3 of II/ZG76, coded M8+XE, Wn 4215, which crashed in the sea at the approximate time in the approximate place, with the crew being rescued by trawler. The pilot, Oblt von Eichborn was badly burned, and his gunner Uffz. Bartmisk killed. In the unlikely event that two twin-engined, twin-finned German aircraft went into the sea in the same area, at the same time, with both crews being picked up by a handy trawler, it would seem that the kill was Norman's, and that the warplane was an Me 110 and not the Dornier he thought it was.

In another skirmish later on the same day, Norman recorded damage to an Me 109. The German fighter streamed glycol under his fire, but with another 109 coming at him from astern, the Derbyshire man had to break away. On that same day – the first of the sprogs to die – PO Ernie Males, with two Me 109s and a Dornier to his credit, was shot down in combat over Sevenoaks. In a letter to his family, Norman wrote of his 'scraps' with the Luftwaffe, recording that he had claimed three kills in five days 'but was unable to keep up (with a view to the DFM!!). I can only hope and wait for a commission some day', he concluded, which was an ambition he richly deserved to fulfill. There was no respite from the conflict – on 29 September his Spitfire was riddled in a clash with 109s: 'Nasty cannon shot in wing, and bullet holes – came back OK though', he reported breezily, adding that he 'saw a 109 crash in pieces. Pilot's chute did not open. Poor sod.' By now the daylight German mass formations had been diluted. Norman commented shrewdly:

Jerry seems to be packing up large formations and going for less bombers and more fighters – swarms of them. They fly very high and we can't get up to them. They come down on us.

By early October, 72 Squadron's combat efficiency was becoming compromised by their losses. The four surviving sprogs badly needed a diversion. Obliged to rely on officers' transport to reach dispersal, a vehicle of their own had become a necessity. A friendly barman advised them of a suitably large limousine lurking in a Bromley garage, and on the 4th they negotiated for the superb 1932 six-cylinder 70bhp Hudson Essex Special Sedan, endowed with a 19hp rating. After some shrewd bargaining, the quartet agreed to purchase it for £19 – £1 per horsepower. Sticky summoned the audacity to ask for a tank-full of petrol, around twenty gallons, and the dealer was sufficiently impressed to allow them three! Norman drove the gleaming blue limousine proudly back to base; it was untaxed and uninsured, but what the hell – they were young and might die at any moment. They bedizened their prize with an RAF roundel on each wing, 'RAF' painted on the windscreen, and fed the monster on a diet of 100-octane fuel. This may well have been the 'large blue car' Norman's younger sister recalled seeing when he came home on leave. Like his Spitfire, it had the name 'Emma' painted on the sides. 'Emma' was ideal for transporting the pilots whom he invited home. Early mornings at leave time involved the family picking their way over sprawled bodies sleeping on settees and armchairs, and a variety of kit – flying boots, jackets, scarves and bags – heaped in the hallway.

Sticky literally paid a flying visit to Derby in the squadron Magister on the 6th, with bad weather delaying his return. On the 7th he was bemoaning his poor deflection shooting. 'Pretty ropey', he called it, 'Must try to improve it!!!' On 8 October he was embroiled in a dogfight at ten in the morning, and his elderly Spitfire K9847 was hit in the glycol tank. With his overheating Merlin crackling and spluttering badly, he belly-landed at Halstead, ploughing through two fields as he went. He recalled being offered by solicitous rescuers: '1. breakfast, 2. lift home, 3. flask of brandy.' He accepted the last and quaffed the contents. An hour later, he was up in the air again. On the 10th another Spitfire rammed his mount, R6777, on the perimeter track, but he was unhurt. It was clear that the entire unit was due for a break and a chance to recuperate in some quiet backwater for a while. Norman's comments became a little irrational. His judgements were perhaps temporarily clouded by his intensive spell of operations. On the day of his collision, he wrote, 'Squadron seems to be cracking up – bad leadership in my opinion' and the next day he criticised the flight leader for refusing to attack a formation of Me 110s. 'Can't understand him', he fulminated, 'we want a fellow who will not break up the squadron.' Piloting X4252 on the 12th, Norman had to return to base as his oxygen supply would not function. He took off again with 92 Squadron, who met a shoal of Me 109s. 'Damaged one, and chased a lot of 'em', he related. A gaggle of bombers escorted 'by hundreds of 109s' were intercepted. 'Whew! Too many for me', he confessed, adding that he 'afterwards chased some Mes and squirted at them'.

72's days at the sharp end had finally run their course and they were recalled to Leconfield, north of Beverley, on 13 October, and 74 Squadron took their place at the Bump. He wrote thankfully, 'Well, I got through it all – might have shot down a few more Huns, but there's plenty of time. Nine original members left out of thirty. What glorious memories and nerve-wracking experiences.' He might have added that with two confirmed victories, plus three shared, two probables and many damaged, he had played no inconsiderable part in the squadron's success. Leconfield was an oasis of peace and quiet, and the rested unit received numbers of fresh pilots for training. Glew's only action was the pursuit of a Dornier 17 on Bonfire Night off Yarmouth. He and Flt Lt Desmond Sheen (Red Section) were vectored onto the bandit at 3.15 p.m., though both were short of fuel after a long patrol. They saw the raider attacking a ship, but it fled down to sea level, with the rear gunner keeping up a constant stream of fire. Glew and Sheen fired at long range, using up most of their ammunition, but the Dornier escaped.

On 8 November Sticky and Gilders were posted to 616 Squadron, and bade a fond and reluctant farewell to the two others sprogs, Rolls and White. Of the four, only Bill Rolls survived the war. The 616 posting, to Kirton-in-Lindsey, lasted just two weeks. The only excitement was a near-miss on the 13th, when he overshot on a night landing with only the Chance light to guide him down. A few days later, he and Gilders moved on to 41 Squadron at Hornchurch.

After a quiet Christmas, 41 began operational sorties over France in their Spitfire Is. Three squadrons took part in an offensive sweep on 10 February. 'France looks so damned peaceful in the sunshine', he wrote. On the 18th the unit inaugurated a system of operating six high-flying Spitfires, deployed in pairs at different heights. The idea was to deter small sections of predatory Me 109s from diving down to pick off RAF fighters operating at lower levels. The first experiment, on 20 February, was a disaster. 'B' Flight were ordered to patrol Maidstone, with Glew piloting P7738. At 20,000 feet he found his hood and windscreen icing-up, and had to break away after informing his leader. He descended to Angels 15, when Control issued an urgent warning of bandits close by. Opening his hood, Sticky climbed back towards his companions, but they had already been attacked by 109s of Stab/JG51, who downed two Spitfires, both despatched by the German ace Werner Molders, with the deaths of both pilots. He saw two Messerschmitts ahead but was unable to get anywhere near them. Incensed by this, he wrote, 'I was left standing, and they were weaving'. Next day brought a stunning shock – the demise of his closest companion, Johnny Gilders, who expired from anoxia, his Spitfire (P7816) crashing at Chilham, Kent, near the banks of the Great Stour River. His body remained in his fighter until its recovery in 1994. The second of the sprogs to go, Johnny's death

A crashed and burnt-out Junkers 87B, which Glew claimed shot down near Benghazi in January 1942. A dislodged and unexploded bomb lies near the starboard wing. (P. Sturdy)

During February 1942, 260 Squadron began re-equipping with Tomahawk IIs. Norman is pictured here in front of one of the aggressive-looking new mounts, AM419. (P. Sturdy)

Within a short time, Kittyhawk Is had supplanted the Tomahawks, and Norman is shown at readiness in the cockpit of one of the new machines (LG 141) at Gasr-el-Arid near Gambut, Libya. The six 0.5 Brownings mounted in the wings provided a devastating punch. Note the back-up ring and bead sight mounted on the upper engine cowling. (P. Sturdy)

devastated Norman, who had little time for grief as he headed home to celebrate the marriage of his elder sister, Jeanne, to Harold Fetch, an army intelligence officer. He imbibed freely at the reception and 'shot a colossal line'.

41 Squadron moved to Catterick and Norman grew bored with the inactivity there. On 13 March he enjoyed himself taking up some of the mechanics in the unit's Magister. On the last trip he performed some aerobatics and the engine suddenly cut out. He just managed to scrape into the airfield with the motor completely dead. That same day his penchant for unauthorised aerobatics got him into hot water with the CO, Sqn Ldr Donald Finlay, who observed him flying across the aerodrome upside-down and 'lowering' his undercarriage whilst inverted, all for a bet. Finlay informed him, 'If you're so keen on flying, you can do night readiness in my place'. He then went to a dance, leaving Sticky 'to stooge about all night, all for being a bad lad'. On 24 March some new Spitfire IIs arrived to supplement the by now obsolescent Mk Is, and Glew set off home for fourteen days' leave.

In April he saw his CO and the Station Commander about the commission he felt he had earned. 'Should have one by now', he complained, 'am brassed off with sergeants' messes.' On the 5th, he drove to Norwich for a weekend with his girlfriend, Peggy. He must have been keen as the journey involved a 220-mile trip in 5 hours! There was little excitement at Catterick; he told his sister that month, 'I spend most of my time looking at the scenery from upside-down'. Consequently, when in early May there was a call for volunteers for a tour overseas, he was quick to sign up.

On 7 May Norman Glew was posted to Drem, Lothian, where he joined 260 Squadron equipped with Hurricane Is. He tried one out on the 10th, enjoying its manoeuvrability but not its relative lack of speed. 'Tried some aerobatics and liked it', he wrote. The squadron were heading abroad and were due to fly long-range Hurricanes from the deck of an aircraft carrier to their destination. After a last binge in Edinburgh, with 'much wine, women and what have you', the unit moved to Scapa Flow in the Orkneys as part of Operation Tracer and embarked on the carrier HMS *Victorious*.

Unfortunately for Norman, the German battleship *Bismarck* chose that moment to appear in the North Atlantic, and instead of their ship heading south to warmer climes, she set off in pursuit of her floating foe, taking 260's pilots and their planes with her. He was livid at the delay. 'I am positively brassed off with the Navy', he raged on the 26th, 'when are we going to fly again?' The next day he was 'absolutely and thoroughly fed up with being afloat. Nothing to do, no exercise, cramped quarters and off food.' One can sympathise with him, knowing he was out in mid-Atlantic in an unfamiliar environment, wondering when and how the operation would end. It ended with the battleship's destruction and, after a short, alcohol-hazed farewell at the Clyde, the carrier set out in earnest for the Mediterranean on 31 May. Norman was allotted Hurricane Z4768, though he felt: 'She will probably be too full of seawater soon to fly off.' *Victorious* anchored at Gibraltar on 11 June, and the pilots enjoyed shore leave, before 260 trans-shipped to the famous *Ark Royal*. At 11 a.m. on the morning of 14 June, with their Hurricanes and Merlins straining at full revs, they took off from the carrier's deck and set course for Malta. A Lockheed Hudson, VX-K of 206 Squadron, took over the navigation to the tiny island, which was four hour's flying time away.

At 3.30 p.m. the Hurricanes landed at Hal Far, on the extreme south of the island, moving on at half-past six the next morning, but soon Z4768's motor began overheating, and Glew had to return to Malta. He flew on the following day to Mersa el Brega, accompanied by a Blenheim. After a cooling bathe at the staging point, he carried on to Suez, which he reached that evening. Since lifting off the *Ark*, he had flown around 1,650 miles. 260 had based themselves at Haifa in Palestine, and on arrival he enjoyed the good food, warmth and sea bathing available in the territory. Tel Aviv appealed to him, and in Jerusalem he tucked into strawberries and cream, as well as oranges, before discussing a commission with the AOC. Afterwards, he 'spent a boozy evening at an RAF dance and met some pretty Jewesses, frigid though', he complained.

On 30 June, Sticky flew to Amman in Trans-Jordan with his unit. In early July the squadron were busy flying sweeps over Syria, hitting Vichy French airfields. On the 4th they refuelled at Damascus, strafed a train, and attacked dispersed aircraft at Talia, and Norman damaged an LeO 45 with his eight Brownings. Back at Amman there was some time for local sightseeing, including a visit to Petra, Keats' 'rose-red city half as old as time'. On the 9th he flew a long mission, refuelling at Damascus and Palmyra, before hitting Aleppo in northern Syria. There were twenty aeroplanes on the 'drome, and he reported setting a large Farman transport ablaze (probably an LeO 257bis which was burnt out). Smoke from the burning aircraft rose to 1,200 feet. He expended the rest of his ammunition on a Potez 63, which he claimed as damaged. On the following day, after a Blenheim escort to Baalbek, Sticky helped machine-gun the airfield petrol dumps, starting two large fires. Shortly afterwards, the Vichy collaborationists sued for peace, and Norman's unit returned to Haifa and its many pleasures. 'What a life!' he commented, as he sampled the attractions on offer. Regrettably, his diaries peter out on 2 August, and only surviving letters and photographs serve as milestones to chart the remainder of his RAF career. On the 22nd he was finally granted a well-justified commission as a pilot officer in the RAFVR.

Norman remained with 260 Squadron until May 1942, during which time they moved from Palestine to the Western Desert, exchanging their outmoded Hurricanes first for Curtiss Tomahawks, then for Kittyhawks. A keen photographer, he collected a number of snapshots covering the period from his posting to the unit to his leaving it. Since 260's combat reports do not survive, and their ORB is not particularly comprehensive, details of his aerial encounters are scanty. On 2 January, still flying a Hurricane, he damaged an Me 109F when his squadron provided top cover on a wing sweep over Agedabia. On the 18th he fired on a Junkers 88, unfortunately without seeing the result. A photograph in his collection shows a crashed and burnt-out Junkers 87B, on the reverse of which he had written: 'Jan '42. A *Stuka* dive bomber with bags of blood in the cockpit. I shot it down near Benghazi. The crew went to a perishing end – though they were not cold by any means'. The date and combat are not specified, but the kill brought his tally of confirmed victories to four, the last one being his victim of 27 September 1940. He also had claims for three shared destroyed and no less than six damaged. Only one more claim has been traced: he damaged an Me 109F on 2 April, while flying a Kittyhawk in an interception of Junkers 87s and their escorts north-west of Tobruk. In a letter to his family he described the termination of his service with 260:

Just before I left, the CO said I was having a flight, which meant becoming an Acting Flt Lt, but I got very badly mauled by a lot of 109s, and this on top of my two years' fighting without a rest rather finished me off. The Doc said I HAD to have a rest. Since then all the boys but me have been killed. Five Sergeant Pilots were commissioned and made Flt Lts straight away, but all were bumped off in rapid succession. They were damned good lads and came out with 260 last year. So perhaps it was a good thing when I was sent on a rest.

The incident referred to occurred on 26 March, when 109s 0f 3/JG27 attacked 260 who were top cover to Bostons returning to Tobruk after a raid on Marturba. Sticky's warplane suffered considerable damage in the combat. The horrendous attrition rate suffered by the squadron reflects the lack of judgement on the part of a high command which left so many fine pilots operating machines unfit to live in the same skies as the Me 109F and the Macchi 202.

From 260 Sticky moved to an Aircraft Delivery Unit, ferrying a variety of military planes from the Maintenance Units to the squadrons. He thought it was interesting, if not exciting, and a great change

Left: *Taken from the cockpit of Glew's Kittyhawk, this photograph shows a strafe against an unidentified target, with a fuel dump ablaze. Note the three Brownings mounted in the leading edge of the fighter's starboard wing.* (P. Sturdy) Right: *Pilot Officer Glew, in unfamiliar blue, is snapped off-duty in Alexandria in March 1942.* (J. Jackson)

Norman examines a captured Macchi C202 Folgore of 96 Squadriglia. The camouflage scheme, one of twenty-five authorised by the Regia Aeronautica, is noteworthy, as is the sideways-hinging canopy, and the access flap for the port-wing machine gun. A souvenir hunter has already cut away the insignia from the rudder to add to his collection. (P. Sturdy)

from his former posting, where he calculated he had been stationed at thirty-six bases. 260 had moved twenty-six times in the year that he spent with them, which is an average of one change a fortnight. He was quite happy abroad and had no wish to return home until the Second Front had been opened. He also managed to spend some time in Egypt's fleshpots, preferring Alexandria to Cairo; he described the former as 'A wizard city – it has Cairo whacked for climate, food and entertainment'. In the latter, which he eschewed because of the drain on his purse, he added yachting to his accomplishments. In two months with the Cairo Yacht Club, he had two firsts and two seconds in races. 'But then', he added, disparagingly, 'the competition were mostly pongoes'. The attractions of Alexandria included a lady friend. He told one sister in October 1942 that he had:

> *... found a wizard girl in Alex. She's Greek, but looks English with lovely blonde hair and a wizzo figure. Am not seriously interested, of course! We go swimming and dancing together when I get up that way.*

He continued ferrying aeroplanes and included a spot of instructing 'which I enjoy immensely' until mid-1943, by which time he was wearing the twin rings of a flight lieutenant. In the July of that year he joined 229 Squadron as a flight commander, flying Spitfires from Qrendi in Malta. He subsequently served with the unit at Hal Far, and Catania in Sicily. On 12 March 1944, after a three-year stint in the Middle East without once seeing home, he was promoted to the rank of squadron leader, and was posted to command 1435 Squadron, stationed at Brindisi near the heel of Italy. He was rightly proud of his advancement, and certain his family would be 'as happy as I am over the promotion for I have never gone out for it but have actually earned it.'

Norman led his new unit for just over two months, gaining the respect and friendship of his pilots. 'They really liked him immensely', wrote his brother-in-law, Harold Fetch, who met the flying personnel of 1435 in late May. 'They'd all such confidence in him as he was way and above the finest pilot & most experienced of them all.' At 11 a.m. on the morning of 17 May, Sticky climbed into the cockpit of Hurricane I KX929. Though 1435 flew Spitfires, they kept the Hawker fighter as a trainer and hack, and he liked to put the machine through its paces occasionally.

He took off with a Spitfire in company, intent on a spot of aerobatics – 'just to keep my eye in', as he remarked immediately before the flight. The two fighters began circling in opposite directions, watched by a number of airmen, all keen to appreciate a show laid on by a skilful veteran. As though at a signal they turned in to one another, twisting and chasing in an effort to get on each other's tail. Banking steeply, Norman went into a very tight turn at low level and the resulting accident occurred with appalling suddenness. He closed too rapidly on his squadron mate and, in a desperate attempt to avoid a collision, pulled up hard. KX929, engine stuttering, stalled away and went into a dive, with Sticky desperately trying to lift up the fighter's nose. He very nearly managed it. If they had had another ten feet of height, his skill would have pulled it off. As it was, the Hurricane dug in its nose at the extreme edge of the airfield, smashed itself into wreckage in a cloud of dust and killed the pilot instantly. Overhead his companion circled, waggling his wings uncertainly at the swiftness of the disaster.

The ambulance was on the spot immediately and Norman's body was removed. Fortunately the aircraft did not catch fire. A few months previously, he had written of his increasing fatalism. 'You just have a card', he stated, 'which the Orderly Angel looks at each day.' On the 17th, his own card had been dealt from the pack. Much earlier, he had noted in his diary: 'It's great fun beating up places, but you have to be careful as the Hurricane cushions downwards when you pull her out'. Had this been a final, despairing thought as he struggled to level out his wallowing warplane? The sad, supreme irony was that he had endured so much real danger, only to perish, like so many others, in a tragic accident.

Norman was buried with full military honours in a quiet Italian cemetery, full of yew trees and flowers, near Brindisi. His fellow officers acted as bearers, the Group Captain was present to pay his respects, and the AOC sent his car, pennant flying, as his representative. His brother-in-law, Harold Fetch, then serving in Italy, was given permission by his CO to drive to Brindisi when he heard of Norman's death, and he wrote a poignant letter to his parents-in-law, setting out the full facts. A brutal reminder of the tragedy was the twisted remains of the Hurricane, still lying at the perimeter of the airfield where it had hit. The Adjutant, Flt Lt James Lamb, who also found time to correspond with his late CO's parents, extolled 'his cheerful personality and ability which made him both a good comrade and an excellent leader'.

Squadron leader Norman Vipan Glew lies buried today at Bari Military Cemetery, 60 miles south-east of Brindisi. It is a truism that the best and finest of a generation often meet their deaths in war. As a volunteer and a first-rank fighting man, Norman certainly fulfils the demands of that category. It is a disgrace that he was never decorated for his unstinting service, although he was not alone, as the combat careers of other Derbyshire stalwarts testify. He had told his sisters more than once that if he had to die, he would be happiest going in a fighter plane. Harold Fetch expressed this in 'one of the saddest things he ever had to write':

The very last thing he would want is for us to be miserable – he would have hated that – he was always so happy and full of spirit – you know flying was in his heart and he lived for it, and I guess that's the way he preferred to die if it had to be. Just think of him in his 'plane and that it was he and his fellow pilots, that, assuredly, have brought us victory. They grow fewer, but their memory lives for always – the salt of the earth.

Who could have put it better?

nine

Pilot Officer
Frank Mellor
DFM

Combat Record

Date	Sqn	Locality	Aircraft Flown	Enemy Type	Claim
17.02.43	111	Pont du Fahs	Spitfire VC JK310	Messerschmitt 109F	Damaged
24.02.43	111	E. Beja	Spitfire VC JK310	Focke-Wulf 190	Destroyed (shared)
28.02.43	111	N.E. Beja	Spitfire VC JK310	Messerschmitt 109F	Destroyed (shared)
04.03.43	111	Beja	Spitfire VC	Messerschmitt 109F	Damaged
05.03.43	111	Hamman Lif	Spitfire VC JG914 JU-I	Messerschmitt 109F	Destroyed (shared)
20.04.43	111	S. Bizerta	Spitfire VC JG806	Messerschmitt 109F	Damaged
01.05.43	111	E. Ras Zebib	Spitfire VC JG806	Messerschmitt 110C	Probable
06.05.43	111	La Marsa	Spitfire VC JG806	Messerschmitt 109F	Destroyed
24.06.43	111	Cape Passaro	Spitfire IX EN518	Messerschmitt 410	Destroyed

This is the only known photograph of Frank. He is bartering for eggs with a Tunisian Arab in the spring of 1943.
(Squadron Archives)

Pilot Officer Frank Mellor DFM

UNFORTUNATELY, LITTLE is known about Frank Mellor's origins and early life, as no friends or relatives have come forward to establish details of his pre-service career. We have only the bare bones on which to build, and background information is therefore very tenuous. He was born in Whaley Bridge in September 1921, to George Arthur Mellor, a stone quarrier, and his wife, Lucy. At the time of his enlistment in the RAF in February 1941, the family were resident in the spa town of Buxton in the High Peak. Frank was accepted for training as a pilot, and joined No.4 ITW at Bexhill, before his posting to Canada, one of the many thousands who received their wings as part of the vast Empire Air Training scheme in the Dominion. By September 1941 he was at No.31 EFTS, Ontario, progressing to 31 SFTS in November, where he became a fully-fledged pilot.

Frank was back in England in February 1942, where he kicked his heels at No.3 Personnel Reception Centre before a posting to No.5 AFU, followed by an eventual move to 5 OTU at Debden. Here, he achieved proficiency in flying modern fighter aircraft. His first operational posting was to 165 Squadron as a sergeant pilot. Within a fortnight he was on the move to Treble One – 111 Squadron – stationed at Kenley under the command of the Battle of Britain veteran, Tony Bartley, who had served with Philip Sanders in 92 Squadron at Biggin Hill in 1940. In late October the unit embarked from the River Clyde for Gibraltar, arriving there on 6 November, a few days after Catapilot Norman Taylor had despatched a Focke-Wulf Condor not too far from the convoy's route. 111's crated Spitfire VCs were assembled, fitted with long-range petrol tanks, and flew off for Maison Blanche, Algiers, on the 11th of the month.

Treble One's introduction to North Africa was not a happy one. The unit was moved forward to the front line, where for many months they operated their Spitfires from muddy airfields, often against superior numbers of enemy raiders, and without the initial benefit of radar to warn of incoming attacks. This necessitated the provision of standing patrols, in addition to the other duties required of the squadron. A temporarily worn-out Bartley relinquished command in January 1943, and Sqn Ldr J.J. Leroux took over from him.

Frank made his first combat claim on 17 February, just over two years after he had joined up. By this time the unit were flying from Waterloo, which was one of the many airstrips dotted around Souk el Khemis in Tunisia. At 2.05 p.m. on that day, six Spitfires of 111 were escorting two Tac R Spitfires from 225 Squadron over Pont du Fahs, with twelve more from 93 Squadron acting as top cover. Unfortunately Mellor's combat reports are not extant, but it is known that on the return flight two Focke-Wulf 190s from 11/JG2 and a single Messerschmitt 109F launched an attack. One of the FWs was shot down, and Frank, piloting JK310, damaged the 109. This aircraft was also fired at by one of the Tac R machines, who saw its right undercarriage leg drop down. The 'Y' Service later heard the German pilot ask permission to bale out, and the Derbyshire flyer seems unlucky not to have been granted at least a half-share in a kill.

Seven days later, again piloting JK310, Frank was one of four 111 flyers who took off at 3.15 p.m. to maintain a standing patrol east of Beja. The fighters became embroiled in a dogfight with FW 190s, and Frank and the section leader, Flt Lt Hill, both scored hits on one of the German warplanes, which was claimed destroyed. He was awarded a half-share in the joint victory. Four days later, still piloting the same Spitfire, he was in the air at 3.15 p.m., helping to escort eight Hurribombers who were attacking enemy tanks and mechanised transport north-west of Beja. Six Mk IX Spitfires from 72 Squadron provided top cover. North-east of the target area, a single foolhardy 109F tried to butt in, and was speedily dealt with by Mellor, assisted by Hill and Sgt Spranger. Each pilot was allotted a third-share in the kill, and the doomed German flyer may have been Ofw. Kolb of 1/JG53, lost near Beja on that day.

Treble One's continuous action was maintained throughout early March. On the 4th of the month, nine of the squadron's fighters provided top cover to two Tac R Spitfires over the Jefna and Sedjen areas, with aircraft from 243 Squadron acting as a medium screen. 111 were vectored on to bandits over Beja, seeing around fifteen to twenty Junkers 87 dive-bombers of 11/StG3 at 9,000 feet, with ten escorting Me 109Fs 5,000 feet higher. The *Stukas* immediately turned for home, bombs tumbling away as they were speedily jettisoned. Some of the British pilots got in among the bombers, and Mellor recorded strikes on an accompanying Me 109F.

Waterloo remained the unit's base throughout the spring, with 111 flying many missions from there in support of the Allied advance. An offensive sweep on 5 April was carried out at 2.20 p.m. by forty-six Spitfires from 72, 93, 111 and 243 Squadrons, led by Wg Cdr 'Sheep' Gilroy. Frank's unit attacked some coastal vessels off Hamman Lif. They were still low down over the Mediterranean coast when a gaggle of nine Me 109Fs bounced them. One Spitfire from 111 was shot down in flames, and the pilot baled out. Three other Spitfires were damaged, with one force-landing on return to their airstrip. To balance the account, Mellor, flying JG914 JU-I, and Sgt Allen dealt with one of the Axis fighters, Uffz. Palmedo of 1/JG53, whose warplane went in south of Hamman, killing the pilot. Frank chalked up a second half-kill to add to his growing total. On the 20th of the month, flying Spitfire JG806 south of Bizerta, he claimed damage to another Me 109F. Presumably this action occurred during a freelance sweep at 4.25 p.m. when Treble One encountered Messerschmitts at 14,000 feet south of the town. The unit claimed two probables and a further 109 damaged.

On May Day at 3.00 p.m. 111 squadron, its aircraft fitted with long-range tanks, flew a patrol over the Gulf of Tunis, with Frank piloting JG806. They went out at nought feet and east of Ras Zebib spotted a formation of 15 Messerschmitt 110s and eight 109s, also skimming the ground on their way to Tunis. The Spitfires rid themselves of their drop-tanks and waded in, with Mellor hammering one of the *Zerstörers*, the first twin-motor enemy warplane he had ever encountered. He claimed a probable – one of a unit total of seven bandits destroyed, plus two probables and two damaged. In the wild, low-level, free-for-all he and FO Pertwee nearly came to grief, touching wings, fortunately only slightly, in the fast-moving clash. The carnage inflicted on the foe raised Treble One to the position of top-scoring squadron in 324 Wing, with forty-eight and five-sixth confirmed victories.

Five days later Frank scored another success, again flying JG806. At 7.50 a.m. the squadron was ordered to patrol La Sebala. They sighted Axis fighters which they chased to La Marsa, where the delighted pilots saw further enemy aircraft landing at the airfield. The squadron diary described the pancaking machines as 'odd-looking types' but they seem to have been Me 109Fs. Frank came down behind one hapless enemy aeroplane as it hung above the landing strip, with its wheels and flaps down. After two short bursts from his cannon, his unfortunate victim crashed in flames. 111's claims on this day gave them the honour of becoming the first RAF unit to top fifty victories in the campaign, despite the fact they still flew Spitfire Vs, when others operated the superior Mk IX. The following day, Frank's dedication and commitment were rewarded by his promotion to the rank of pilot officer.

On 13 May, which was the day of the final Axis capitulation, 111 flew to Protville 1, north-west of Tunis, and moved on to Mateur, south-west of Bizerta, twelve days later. The squadron ended its operational service in Tunisia by flying standing patrols over the capital while it was being occupied. On 10 June, after a hard and gruelling six months, often under unfavourable conditions, the unit moved to Safi on Malta, earning a short respite before the rigours of the forthcoming assault on Sicily. By this time the battle-worn Mk Vs were being replaced by IXEs, a type they were destined to retain until 1947!

In preparation for the attack on the island, 111 flew their new mounts in almost daily sweeps, strafing and escorting bombing raids. On the morning of 24 June at 11 a.m. a section of patrolling Spitfires from Treble One were vectored on to that rarest of rare birds, a brand-new Messerschmitt 410 twin-engined reconnaissance aircraft of 2(F)122, based at Trapani. The unlucky lone bandit was sighted at sea-level off Cape Passaro on the south-east coast of Sicily, and PO Mellor, flying EN518, was the first to intercept. Frank blasted the slender target from close range, seeing return fire from the rear gunner Uffz. Weber, before the hapless quarry, coded F6+XE, plunged into the sea. Weber and his pilot, Obltn. Nauck, both perished in the crash. The victory was Frank's final combat kill.

Frank flew Spitfire VCs similar to this Supermarine warplane, which is warming up for take-off on a Tunisian airstrip in early 1943. The bulk of these fighters still carried the drag-inducing Vokes air filters.

Mellors' main antagonists in Tunisia were the formidable Messerschmitt 109Fs, like the one shown here. Frank claimed one destroyed, and shared in two further kills.

141

Opposite above: *Frank's other main opponent was the Focke-Wulf 190A, which was similar to the one preserved here at the Imperial War Museum in London.* (Author)

Opposite below: *The Messerschmitt 410 was a* rara avis. *Frank shot one down off Cape Passaro, in Sicily. It was his last combat victory.*

Left: *A larger version of the picture on page 138 shows the distant Spitfires of 111 Squadron acting as a backdrop to Frank's bartering as the purchasing agent for the unit.*

Below: *A 109F in tropical war paint is preserved at Duxford Air Museum in Cambridgeshire.* (Author)

On 3 July, piloting Spitfire IX EN259, Frank was one of an eight-fighter escort covering the 'Spitbombers' of 126 Squadron in a diversionary raid on Biscari airfield. Three 1Xs, led by Wg Cdr Hugh 'Cocky' Dundas, with Frank as one of his wingmen, provided top cover, with the other six Spitfire Vs acting as close escort. The formation took off at 3.40 p.m., and the accurate bombing, at 4.15 p.m., was unopposed. However, as the Spitbombers pulled away from the target, over twenty Me 109Fs and Macchi C202s intercepted the formation. Half the bandits made a feint attack on the escort, apparently attempting to draw them away from their charges, before turning to attack the fighter-bombers. The other enemy aircraft went straight for the escorts, and in the ensuing mêlée the 111 pilots claimed two 109s destroyed, plus two damaged.

During the combat, Frank's Spitfire took hits in the engine. He and Dundas turned for home, and over the Sicilian coast, the few pursuing Messerschmitts pulled away and left them in peace. Dundas saw a thin stream of white vapour dragging behind his companion's aeroplane, and called Frank on the R/T to tell him that his coolant system had been punctured. Frank replied that his engine temperature was on the rise. Both fighters were flying at 16,000 feet and the Wing Commander thought there was a good chance of getting the wounded bird back to Malta. 'I throttled back', he wrote, 'told him to follow close beside me and concentrated on steering the best possible course and on flying in such a way that we would cover the distance as quickly as possible, but with the minimum use of power.' Unfortunately the 111 Squadron CO, George Hill, chose this moment to radio Dundas to say that he was circling a manned dinghy 2 or 3 miles south of Cape Passaro. He asked for assistance as predatory 109s were gathering nearby. By this time Malta was in sight only 15 miles away, and Dundas called Control and asked them to warn Air Sea Rescue to ready themselves for a pickup. He then left Mellor to carry on to base by himself, ordering him to bale out if his engine temperature rose above 125 degrees. He would, Dundas believed, be rescued without difficulty if he were forced to hit the silk. Dundas then joined Hill, and aided him in repelling the waiting Messerschmitts. The pair eventually made Malta with their petrol tanks all but dry, only to find that Frank Mellor had failed to reach the island. Although Dundas did not mention the fact in his book *Flying Start,* Frank was missing, and around twenty-four Spitfires from various units flew out to search for him. They located a dinghy, but to their disgust when HSL107 arrived to rescue the pilot, they found that the occupant was only 'a Hun'.

What happened to Frank can only be conjecture. Either he crashed into the sea or baled out of his ailing warplane and drowned. His body was in due course recovered off the Sicilian coast, and was buried at Catania War Cemetery on the east coast of the island. The squadron diary, in regretting his death, described him as 'one of our most valuable pilots'. Almost a year later, a Distinguished Flying Medal was gazetted for the Derbyshire airman, which was effective from the day before his death. The citation recorded that he was 'a splendid example to the men of his squadron'. During his short combat career, Frank was credited with two enemy aircraft destroyed, plus three shared destroyed, with one probable and three damaged. Sadly, we know so little about Frank on a personal level, but surviving personnel of Treble One endorse the general high opinion of the tall and proficient flyer, with his tousled fair hair, whose only likeness so far known shows him bartering for eggs with a local arab near a Tunisian airfield, with the Spitfires of his unit forming an appropriate backdrop. One hopes there is still someone left to mourn this gallant young warrior and keep his memory in mind.

ten

Wing Commander Frank Geoffrey Woolley DFC and bar AFC

Combat Record

Date	Sqn	Locality	Aircraft Flown	Enemy Type	Claim
02.07.44	602	S.E. Caen	Spitfire IX ML307 LO-V	Focke-Wulf 190D	Damaged
14.02.45	41	Rheinie	Spitfire XIV RM791 EB-V	Focke-Wulf 190D	Probable
13.03.45	350	Hamm	Spitfire XIV NH686 MN-V	Focke-Wulf 190D	Destroyed
24.04.45	130	S. Wismar	Spitfire XIV AP-T	Messerschmitt 108	Destroyed
25.04.45	130	Pritzwalk	Spitfire XIV AP-T	Siebel 204	Destroyed
30.04.45	130	N. Lauenberg	Spitfire XIV AP-T	Focke-Wulf 190A	Destroyed

A youthful Frank poses in front of an Audax trainer at 4FSTS, Habbaniyah in Iraq, late in 1940.
(J. Woolley)

Wing Commander Frank Geoffrey Woolley DFC and bar AFC

FRANK WOOLLEY, not to be confused with the famous cricketing all-rounder of pre-war days, but equally as proficient in his chosen profession as the man of Kent, was born in Ilkeston in June 1922, the son of Frank Woolley and Gladys, née Willgoose. His father was a serving officer in the RAF, the son of Alderman Joseph Woolley JP of Ilkeston. Both Franks proudly wore the ribbon of the Distinguished Flying Cross before they reached the age of twenty, and Frank junior was the most decorated of all Derbyshire fighter pilots in the Second World War. Frank was not strictly an ace, but with four confirmed kills, plus one probable and one damaged was within a mathematical fraction of that coveted status, and as such surely deserves inclusion within these pages, alongside his equally distinguished parent.

The father and son theme is very strong in the Woolley story. Both were fighter pilots, and the father taught the son to fly. They both clashed with enemy aircraft in the skies over Europe in different wars, and Frank senior claimed nine victories, four destroyed and five out-of-control, whilst flying Sopwith Dolphins with 79 Squadron in 1918. He was decorated personally with the Croix de Guerre by the Belgian King in 1919. His story is told in the author's *Winged Warriors,* published in 2003. From his early days, young Frank was indoctrinated into a military atmosphere. 'They live and talk in air force terms in the Woolley household', wrote a later newspaper scribe, and it was presumably understood that he would follow in his father's footsteps when the time came for him to choose his career. In fact, he intended to go to Cranwell, but when war broke out the College closed. Desperately keen to learn to fly, he became tired of 'stooging around', waiting to volunteer. He wrote to his father, who was then serving in Malaya, asking permission to join him by working his passage to the Far East, where he could hopefully take the necessary instruction. His father sent him a cheque to subsidise the voyage, and Frank subsequently joined him in Singapore.

Frank junior joined the Singapore Flying Club and his father undertook his *ab initio* training in an Avro Tutor. Young Woolley, who was short and slender, was a natural – 'born to fly' – and his father thought him competent to solo after 4 hours and 10 minutes of instruction. However, he deferred the moment until he had given his son a careful and comprehensive grounding in every aspect of basic flying training. Frank duly gained his 'A' Licence and was posted to No.4 Anti-Aircraft Co-operation Unit at Kallang in early July. In September he was granted one of six vacancies allotted by the Air Ministry to Malayan 'A' Licence holders to undertake further training in Iraq. He joined No.4 FSTS at Habbaniya, south-east of Baghdad, where he polished up his flying on a series of training aircraft and worked so hard at ground subjects that he was awarded a distinction.

The eighteen-year-old was commissioned as a pilot officer on 29 March 1941, and was posted to 244 Squadron stationed at Shaibah near Basra. 244 was a general purpose unit, and Frank may well have been somewhat nonplussed by the squadron mounts which were Vickers Vincents, variants of the torpedo-carrying Vildebeests. These archaic machines were clumsy-looking and incredibly ugly biplanes with a 50-foot wingspan and a massive fixed, spatted undercarriage. They carried a crew of up to three, a fixed front gun and a flexible rear one, and could haul an external 1,000lb bomb load. This amazing contraption was powered by a 650hp Pegasus radial motor, driving a huge two-blade wooden airscrew, which dragged the aeroplane along at a top speed of 140mph. The one bonus to flying these airborne dinosaurs was the superb view enjoyed by the pilot as he bumbled across the landscape.

Woolley went into action far sooner than he would have thought, and not against his expected foes, but the Iraqis. The Axis had established a pro-German government in the country, and to protect her treaty rights, Britain landed a brigade from India on 18 April, under the command of General Wavell. The Iraqis responded by besieging the RAF base at Habbaniya, but the British held command of the air, and by concentrated attacks forced the enemy to retreat. Wavell followed up by launching an assault on Baghdad, which fell on 30 May, effectively ending the war.

Flight Lieutenant Frank Woolley DFC after the presentation of his first decoration at Buckingham Palace, in autumn 1943. (J. Woolley)

After spending the early weeks with his unit on training missions and escort patrols, Frank flew his first operation on 2 May. It was a two-plane sortie to bomb the railway line 60 miles south-west of Ur, around 100 miles from base. He piloted Vincent K4732, with LAC Howard as his observer, carrying four 250lb bombs to hopefully disrupt the Iraqi rail system. To judge from his logbook, the raid was completely routine, with no clue that this was the mission on which he gained his first DFC. This was entirely in keeping with Woolley's laconic and taciturn character, and his feeling that he was just a man doing a job. As the Vincents sighted the railway, they noticed an armoured train loaded with troops on the line, and manoeuvred to release their bombs on this opportune target. As they pulled out of their runs with bombs gone, Frank's companion aircraft, K6365, piloted by Flt Lt G.B. Haywood, suddenly lurched away, either struck by ground fire or, as other accounts suggest, damaged by the blast of its own bombs. It staggered along, with its engine gradually dying, and smashed into the ground not far from the track that they had been attacking. Circling the wreckage, Woolley made the decision to land and try to rescue the injured crew of the downed warplane. The ground, sandy and rock-strewn, looked most unsuitable for the purpose but, helped by the robust and massive undercarriage, he managed to put K4732 down near the broken remnants of the other machine. He and Howard hastily dragged the two aircrew out of their shattered cockpits, administered rudimentary first aid, and stowed them in the fuselage.

Suddenly bullets began whistling around the Vincent as Iraqi soldiers appeared in the distance, anxious, as all bombed and strafed infantry are, to interview their attackers. To his dismay, Frank found that his aircraft's wheels were stuck in the soft sand. With the enemy only a few hundred yards away, he leapt into his cockpit and revved up the idling Pegasus motor, as Howard deterred the advancing soldiery by bursts from his Lewis gun. The huge propeller whipped up a miniature sandstorm, aided by the fierce slipstream and the pilot's action in swinging the aeroplane from side to side by means of the large rudder. The bemused Iraqis, unable to see their target and engulfed by the stinging sandblasts, watched helplessly as the ponderous aircraft taxied out of the soft sand on to a stretch of firmer ground. Heart in mouth, Woolley opened his throttle and the lumbering Vincent slowly came unstuck and climbed away to safety. He returned his wounded colleagues to Shaibah, without doubt saving their lives. The only comment in his logbook was the pencilled phrase 'shakey do', which in its way is one of the classic one-liners in RAF history!

Frank Woolley was awarded an almost immediate DFC for his amazing exploit, but getting the story out of him was rather like extracting teeth. One colleague wrote, 'He himself has been entirely uncommunicative in regard to the exploit', and Frank wrote to his father, 'It was nothing at all. I didn't believe it when they told me. They will no doubt have to post me now so that I can earn it.' In reality, Woolley's action was almost cold-bloodedly courageous, a calculated decision which saved two fellow airmen and thoroughly deserved the results it merited. One can only hope that the other hero, LAC Howard, received some credit for his not inconsiderable part in the affair.

244 Squadron continued to support the British forces in the Middle East. By late August they were overflying Iran, which the British and Russians occupied on the 25th, to forestall a possible Axis coup. By this time, Frank was an acting flying officer, and perhaps at the time the youngest flight commander in the RAF. On the 26th he was wounded in the leg when his Vincent K6366 was shot down by an apparently myopic Hurricane pilot of 261 Squadron, while on an Army co-operation mission to Ahwaz. The aircraft force-landed 10 miles south of its target and was duly burned, while he and his observer, Sgt Featherstone, were rescued by the cavalry – the motorised 17th Lancers picked them up and returned them safely to the British lines.

After a period of hospitalisation in Basra, Frank rejoined 244, and served with the unit until April 1942. He was given some overdue leave and visited his father in Colombo, Ceylon, where the latter was then stationed. In the autumn of 1942, he returned to England to train as a fighter pilot. He joined 57 OTU at Hawarden near Chester, completing the course with an 'Above Average' assessment. He remarked on the good parties at Chester: 'Service life is a hell of a change from Iraq' he wrote. He flew Spitfires whilst at the OTU, and by early December he felt very much at home in the fighter, with his air-firing average being the highest on the course. It was quite a change from the sluggish old Vincents with which he had started the war!

Frank was posted to 132 Squadron, flying Spitfire VBs from Martlesham. They performed the usual duties that fell to UK-based fighter units during the period – convoy patrols, bomber escorts, 'Rodeos' and 'Ramrods'. He saw enemy aircraft on occasion, but never got to grips with them. He enjoyed life with 132, commenting on the 'bags of popsies and good beer'. He developed that affinity with his aeroplane (FF-J for most of the summer) that many fighter pilots shared. 'Whenever I am away from the squadron', he wrote to his father in July, 'I worry like hell what I am missing and what is happening to my kite. It is amazing to think how one can have so much affection for an inanimate thing like an aircraft.'

In August he went on a fighter leaders' course at the School of Tactics, Charmy Down, reporting a 'shakey do' on the 17th whilst flying Spitfire GK-N. 'My motor clapped out 15 miles over the wet', he wrote. 'I just managed to stagger back to the shore and force-land on an aerodrome (Fairwood Common) which was very conveniently there.' He returned to 132, but on 1 November was posted as 'B' Flight commander to 602 Squadron, AAF, flying Spitfire IXBs. The unit contained many notable characters within its ranks, and its operations in the middle-war years were chronicled by the Frenchman Pierre Clostermann in his best-seller, *The Big Show*. The CO was 'Maxie' Sutherland, who made Frank more than welcome. The Derbyshire man continued his war very much as with 132 Squadron, with the added spice produced by a series of exhilarating, if dangerous, 'rhubarbs' and escort cover operations for USAAF Flying Fortresses returning from deep penetration

This is a Vickers Vincent, which is similar to the ones Woolley flew in offensive operations over Iraq and Iran during 1941. This particular machine is being flown by his father, who was also an RAF pilot. (J. Woolley)

Frank pilots Audax K3714 in this fine air-to-air shot taken over the Iraqi countryside. (J. Woolley)

raids. The Christmas of 1943 was notable because of a generous present from the unit's home city, Glasgow, whose well-wishers provided a case of forty-five-year-old whisky and 60 gallons of Algerian wine. Not surprisingly, Frank informed his parents he would not be taking Christmas leave that year!

Woolley had a narrow escape early in the New Year whilst flying LO-O (MH972), acting as high cover for RP Hurricanes attacking Ligescourt. He was hit in the engine by ground fire, with one bullet tearing a hole in his Merlin's magneto casing. Fortunately he was able to nurse his mount home. On the 4th, which was the next day, whilst piloting LO-W on a 'ramrod', escorting 72 Marauders to Amiens, the bombers managed to lose themselves, resulting in an 'inevitable Cook's tour of France'. 602 had a short sojourn at Skeabrae in the frozen Orkneys from 18 January, and 'B' Flight were less than pleased when they were shunted even further north to the even less hospitable Shetlands. Here, they lost their Spitfire IXs, and reverted to LFVs – 'cropped, clipped and clapped', as he described them in his logbook. Five weeks later the squadron were back in England. He went on a Gyro Gunsight Instructors' course at Southend, before, on 13 March, 602 regained their 1Xs and moved to Llanbedr in Wales for an intensive spell at the Armament Practice Camp. This was in preparation for extra duties allotted to the squadron, whose Spitfires were fitted with racks to carry 500lb bombs. The pilots undertook both dive and level bombing, and air-to-ground firing. Frank emerged with a 'Good Average' all-round performance. In March, 602 moved to Detling, and on 18 April, carried out their first dive-bombing mission, lobbing their single 500-pounders through intense flak at a 'Noball' site, No.78. These sites turned out to be launching complexes for V1 flying bombs, and were heavily pulverised from the air in the run-up to D-Day.

Throughout the late spring and early summer of 1944, Flt Lt Woolley piloted Spitfire ML307 L-OV in an exhausting series of 'ramrods,' 'rodeos' and dive-bombing attacks on various targets. On 2 May, eleven Spitfires of 602 attacked the thirty-nine-arch railway viaduct at Merville, between Paris and Le Havre, diving from 10,000 feet to release their bombs at 3,000, again hurtling through heavy ack-ack fire. They scored two hits on the target. On the 10th Frank opened fire on a German aircraft, for the very first time in eighteen months of combat flying. The mission was a Ramrod, escorting 36 Martin Marauders bombing Creil. The formation was attacked by ten Focke-Wulf 190s, and the Derbyshire flier 'had 3 squirts at one. Range too great. E/A could apparently outrun and outclimb us'.

During May, a number of Noball targets were engaged, with the Spitfires more often than not dive-bombing through intense flak. On escort missions they began carrying 90-gallon drop-tanks to extend their range. On the 30th, with invasion imminent, radar stations were bombed and strafed. One raid, on a site near Arromanches, destroyed the target and inflicted 200 casualties on the enemy. On D-Day, Frank flew LO-V over the bay of the Seine and the Cherbourg peninsula, covering the American invasion beaches and viewing the huge armada operating offshore. No enemy aircraft were seen either on that day or the following two, when 602 provided low cover over the beachhead. On the 13th he saw Caen on fire, and two days later the squadron landed in France for the first time, pancaking at Bazinville ALG. The overnight stay was not appreciated, and Frank commented on being 'bombed and general bloody shambles all night. Airfield worse than the desert.' Further nights were spent on these safaris. 602 took advantage of the French food, wine, cosmetics and silk stockings available from nearby Bayeux, but hated the gunfire which kept them awake all night.

On 21 June, the squadron helped to escort 100 Halifaxes blasting Noball sites near Neufchatel. Three days later they landed at ALG B9, Creully, moving on to B11 at Longues, which was the home of 125 Wing, on the 25th. From this new base, 602 embarked on a series of low-level sweeps, strafing enemy transport. On the 30th, Frank chased an Me 109 which slipped away into cloud. On the afternoon of 2 July, some twenty months after his first operational flight from England, Woolley took part in his first real combat with the Luftwaffe. At 4 p.m. that day, the four aircraft of Blue Section, followed by two of Red (Clostermann and Ken Charney), scrambled south-east of Caen, with Frank leading the formation. 602 had only just returned from a patrol and only a few of the Spitfires had been refuelled. Thick-layered clouds covered the sector through which the six fighters climbed. At 7,000 feet the warplanes levelled off just below a mass of nimbo-stratus, and above them around twenty to thirty enemy aircraft broke through the clouds at 10,000 feet. On seeing the Spitfires below, the German gaggle – long-nosed Focke-Wulf 190Ds – jettisoned their auxiliary petrol tanks and came down to attack.

Frank led his section into a left-hand turn, diving before pulling up in a steep, climbing spiral at full throttle, which led him straight into the whirling mass of enemy aeroplanes. In the mêlée he loosed off several short bursts from his cannon and machine guns, to no effect. Continuing to turn hard to counter the German tactics of dive and climb, he picked out and followed a single 190 above, pulling for the topmost layer at 10,000 feet. On reaching the clouds, he levelled off behind his opponent, finding the layer transparent enough for him to identify the long-nosed outline clearly, like the aircraft silhouettes pinned up in the squadron operations room. At 400 yards, Woolley steadied the luminous orange spot of his gunsight on the image in front, squeezing off a short burst. The 190 immediately began to fishtail in a slow weave. When it straightened, it received a second dose which produced immediate strikes – a bright flash on the port side of the fuselage and a puff of black smoke on the nose cowling. The enemy fighter flicked violently over and disappeared under the nose of Frank's LO-V. Elsewhere, the skies had miraculously cleared of black crosses, and the scattered Spitfires, fortunately unscathed, turned back for home. 'Hell of a scrap', he wrote in his log. The final count was much to 602's credit: two FW 190s destroyed by Clostermann, plus four more damaged by the two sections. Woolley thus opened his account with a modest claim of one FW190D damaged.

Frank's time with 602 was almost over. On his last patrol, on the 4th, his Merlin spluttered to a stop 10 miles south-east of Caen, and he just managed to glide back to base. His faithful LO-V, game to the last, did not let him down. It was his last sortie with 602 and the end of his first tour. He had

Frank stands third from left in this 132 Squadron line-up on and around a clipped-wing Spitfire V in 1943. The fighter stands on a chain-link strip of artificial runway. (J. Woolley)

Woolley is in full flying gear in the 'office' of Spitfire V Ethel Marsden. As far as the author is aware, there is no connection between him and the unknown lady! (J. Woolley)

amassed 993 flying hours, with 242 of them being on Spitfires. On the evening of 7 July, he and Clostermann, also time-expired, embarked for home on LCT 322 from Arromanches, sped on their way by a night-time bombing raid on the port.

Flight Lieutenant Frank Woolley spent the rest of the year with the staff of the Fighter Leader School at Milfield. He left the unit in early January 1945 after a lengthy Christmas celebration – 'One long party from Dec 23 to 27', as he put it – before undertaking a short familiarisation course on the Spitfire XIV. This latest in the line of Supermarine variants was powered by a 2,000hp Griffon 65 motor driving a five-blade propeller, and was potentially the finest fighter available to the Allies in the last year of the war. The Spitfire XIV equipped his new squadron, No.41, to which he was appointed in late January as OC 'A' Flight. 41 Squadron was part of 125 Wing, 2nd TAF, and was stationed at Volkel in Holland, where Woolley renewed his acquaintance with Clostermann, then 'B' Flight Commander in 274 Squadron, flying Hawker Tempest Vs. To start with there was little contact with the Luftwaffe, and the unit spent its time in armed recces, strafing locomotives, enemy transport and 'anything that moves'. Frank told his parents that he was now 'laying off the grog' and found it 'pleasant getting up in the morning *sans* headache'. The weather was cold, but he was billeted in a convent with central heating. He confessed to preferring the Dutch to the French, and in the absence of entertainment spent much time listening to the wireless. 'This sort of life seems to suit me', he wrote.

At 7.45 a.m. on the morning of St Valentine's Day, as Blue 1, flying Spitfire RM791 EB-V, he led two other aircraft in an armed patrol between Lingen and Osnabruck at 3,000 feet. At 8.15 a.m., one mile south of Rheinie airfield – an absolute hotbed of German light AA – he saw some twelve enemy aircraft wheeling in the circuit. Pulling round for a closer look, he observed red Very lights arcing up from the ground, warning the opposition of the danger. Woolley curved round behind a section of three Focke-Wulf 190s circling the locality, but as he closed the range, tracer flashed by

Frank, who is standing second from left, poses with fellow-pilots from 602 Squadron in front of a Spitfire IX in early 1944. Sqdn Ldr 'Maxie' Sutherland is fifth from left, and Pierre Clostermann eighth. (J. Woolley)

him from a fourth 190, some 400 yards astern. The Derbyshire pilot swiftly broke into the threat, causing his pursuer to turn away for the airfield. As he chased the FW round the circuit, intense light flak opened up, speckling the air round the two fighters. Frank flinched as a shell smacked into his tailplane. He discovered later it was a 40mm round, which blew off a large part of his rudder and partly jammed his elevators.

Despite his unpromising position, Frank pressed on grittily, aiming three short bursts at his target from 300 yards. Although he saw no hits, the 190 pulled up sharply in front of him, and two objects fell away. Woolley thought they were the 190's hood, followed by the pilot baling out. The Spitfire flashed underneath the German warplane, which turned over and went down, possibly hit by its own flak. Diving away at under 300 feet, there seems little chance that the machine could recover from what was presumably its death-dive. He could only claim a probable, whilst his number two, FO Gray, was able to damage a Messerschmitt 262 jet fighter which he attacked in the Rheinie circuit. Frank wrote that he had 'diced with 12 FW 190s round Rheinie aerodrome', and had been hit in the tail.

One of the pilots' worst problems was the lack of washing and laundry facilities. The only place for a hot bath was a baker's shop in the village, and it was virtually impossible to get any washing done. However, there were compensations, including mess beer at 4d a pint and spirits at 4d a tot. At the end of February, Frank got his half-stripe, and was posted to command 350 (Belgian) Squadron at Eindhoven. The unit's tasks were mainly 'Rodeos' and 'Ramrods', escorting medium bombers in their Spitfire XIVs. His long-overdue first confirmed kill finally came on 13 March as he was piloting MN-V (NH686) as Black 1, escorting 36 Marauders on a bombing mission. 350 were flying in four independent sections of four aircraft each. At 2.45 p.m. the formation were ten miles north-east of Hamm at 20,000 feet, with the bombers 4,000 feet lower, passing over an eight-tenths cloud layer. Looking down through a gap in the clouds, Woolley saw a cluster of black dots at 12,000 feet, heading in the opposite direction. Snapping out orders over the R/T, he rolled MN-V and plunged after the bogies.

Breaking through the cloud-mass, he identified a loose gaggle of single-engined warplanes one mile ahead. They were moving quickly, and it took him two minutes at full throttle before he caught them up. Not yet certain of their identity, he flew up the starboard side of the group, pulling up alongside the outer machine. As the bogey pulled round into him, he identified it as a long-nose FW 190D, and manoeuvred to get on its tail. The German pilot pulled up his nose and climbed hard to a layer of thin, wispy cloud above. Hanging on behind, Frank framed the 190 in his gunsight and opened fire from dead astern at 100 yards. Bright flashes lit up the wing roots and fuselage of the bandit as his shells struck home. The Focke-Wulf burst into flames as its fuel tanks ignited; fire blossomed out from its port wing root and streamed from the bottom of the cockpit. Chunks of debris broke away from the doomed aircraft, and Woolley had to take sharp evasive action to avoid the whirling fragments. His number two, PO Watkins, saw the CO's victim roll away ablaze, trailing smoke and fire like a comet, as it literally burned itself out in the air.

On 18 March, the unit paid a short visit to Warmwell in Dorset for a bombing and gunnery course. On 10 April, Frank was posted again, this time to command 130 Squadron based at Twente. A fellow pilot in this unit recalled his new CO as 'unassuming ... a born leader and brilliant tactician'. Woolley's pilots carried on the business of patrols and low-level strafing operations, moving to Celle in central Germany on the 17th. Frank was delighted by his quarters here, which were on a former Luftwaffe station. The mess was like an exclusive West End hotel, and he had the luxury of a sitting room and bedroom with a superb divan. The furniture was ultra-modern, and there was a magnificent Telefunken radio to listen to. Evidently, the German Air Force did not believe in stinting its officers!

In his *2nd Tactical Air Force*, Chris Shores recorded that Woolley had to bale out from his aircraft on 19 March, when his Spitfire was hit by a rocket fired from an enemy vessel in Wismar Bay. No such event is recorded, either in his logbook or in the 130 Squadron diary, and doubt must be cast on the authenticity of this occurrence. On the morning of the 24th, he was leading Red Section in Spitfire AP-T on a reconnaissance over Lubeck. South of Wismar at 3,000 feet at 7.15 a.m., he noticed a train crawling over the winter landscape, and was descending to attack when his sharp eye picked out a single aircraft heading north-west at ground level. It was an inoffensive Messerschmitt 108 communications monoplane, with lines similar to the far more potent 109. Frank chased this slippery target round and round with increasing frustration, as his agile opponent sought to escape its fate. Finally, he came in head-on, and a snap burst was rewarded with several bright strikes. The 108 pulled away to force-land in a nearby field, with the CO going down to finish it off. The whole section witnessed the hapless machine blazing on the ground and were able to confirm the kill. Later that day, 130 carried out a 'Rodeo' north of Berlin. They met up with unfamiliar aircraft, which as they closed were seen to carry red stars on their wings and fuselages. 'It was a hell of an occasion', Frank reported in a letter to his father, the RAF and the Red Air Force meeting for the first time ever over enemy territory.

Next day Woolley met another unfamiliar machine. He was again leading Red Section on an armed recce over the Pritzwalk neighbourhood at 2 p.m. in AP-T, at 7,000 feet, when an unidentified twin-motor aeroplane came into sight around 6,000 feet below. Approaching the stranger from above and behind, he recognised the twin-tailed aircraft as a Siebel 204, a five-seater light transport with a stubby body and long, slender wings. Woolley's wretched quarry rapidly succumbed as he bored in, flailing it with cannon and point fives as he closed to fifty yards, with flashes winking all over the fuselage as his bursts hit home. One engine began dragging a long scarf of smoke, and the struggling machine gave up the unequal contest, crashing and burning out in a nearby field.

Frank Woolley's final kill came on the last day of April, with the Third Reich on its last legs and Allied aircraft ranging the length of the Fatherland at will. It occurred on a patrol over the Lauenberg-Elbe bridgehead at 2,000 feet, with the CO once more leading Red Section in AP-T. Just north of Lauenberg, he spotted a short-nosed Focke-Wulf 190 steering west 500 feet above him. Execution was swift; he caught up with the lone German near Winsen at 1.50 p.m. The German pilot sighted the Spitfire, and twisted to port as the pursuer fired a two-second burst at 200 yards, angled off twenty degrees. The aim was sure, and shells and bullets raked the enemy cockpit, gouging out debris from the port-wing root. The pilot obviously dead, large fragments fluttered away from the low-winged monoplane as, flames streaming, it plummeted into a swamp, breaking up in a spray of mud and dirty water.

Frank was obviously just getting into his stride, with three victories in seven days. However, he only met the Luftwaffe on one further occasion. On 2 May, while patrolling Wittenberg-Schwerin in AP-H, the section chased eight 190s and an Me 262. Unfortunately, 'the bastards got away in clouds'. Later that day, his fighter's Griffon engine packed up in the airfield circuit, necessitating a forced landing. His final action followed the next day when he strafed German mechanised transport in AP-C on an armed recce in the Rendlesberg-Keil locality. 130 had maintained a hot pace under Woolley's leadership; during April they had destroyed forty-two enemy aircraft and over 300 vehicles at the low cost of four Spitfires and one pilot. He was rather piqued when on 7 May the unit's Spitfire XIVs were summarily replaced by 'clapped-out IXBs'. On the 10th the squadron were transferred from the 2nd TAF to Fighter Command.

In July, Squadron Leader Woolley was awarded a bar to his DFC. The citation described him as 'a determined and courageous leader, whose ability and skill have been reflected in the success achieved by those serving under him'. It recorded his 'numerous hazardous missions', the destruction of four enemy aircraft in combat, and 77 German vehicles on the ground. It concluded by remarking that:

On many of his flights, severe opposition from the ground has been encountered, but despite the danger, this officer has continued to display outstanding courage and devotion to duty on air operations.

Like his father, Woolley decided to make the RAF his career after the war. He remained the CO of 130 Squadron until July 1946, which included a spell at Kristiansand in Norway, where he

Frank Woolley hangs on to one of the five blades of his Spitfire XIVs propellor at Volkel, 41 Squadron's base, in February 1945. (J. Woolley)

The massive nose and huge five-bladed airscrew of Frank's Griffon-powered Spitfire XIV show up well in this view of his 350 Squadron machine Elizabeth X *at Warmwell in March 1945. (J. Woolley)*

A rare bird was the Siebel 204 twin-motor transport, one of which Woolley despatched on 25 April. It was the day after the destruction of the Me 108.

occasionally flew an ex-German Fieseler Storch. He was then appointed to a permanent commission as a flight lieutenant, and received a Mention in Despatches. In May of that year, the squadron undertook an unusual assignment, when they simulated attacks on Junkers 88s for the otherwise forgettable Two Cities film *School For Secrets,* which starred Ralph Richardson and Richard Attenborough. Frank joined HQ No.11 Group until December 1947; in October he converted onto jet aircraft, with his first familiarisation flight being on a twin-boom Vampire I fighter. Later that year he lost his half-stripe and became a flight commander with 54 Squadron, under the leadership of famous fighter pilot Frank Howell, and after his unfortunate death, Bobby Oxspring. Whilst with this unit, which flew Vampire jets, he took part in a goodwill tour of Canada and the United States.

The tour involved the first-ever crossing of the Atlantic by jet aircraft – six Vampire 3s, flying in two sections of three, each led by a Mosquito as navigator. Two Avro York transports followed with spares and ground-crew. The flight was hazardous, with strong headwinds and cloudbanks up to 40,000 feet. In North America they gave some spectacular displays in Toronto, Trenton, Idlewild and Greenville, South Carolina. Local press accounts referred to them as 'the slickest airborne ambassadors of goodwill you'll ever have a look-see at', praising the 'personable lads' with their 'charm and rugged good looks', who were doing 'a jam up job of cementing international relations'. 54 Squadron's superb skills were appreciated by large crowds; at Greenville, Frank, piloting VT869, led three other Vampires in a virtuoso performance praised as 'the most remarkable precision flying in aviation history here'. The visit was a huge success, and Woolley's performances were doubtless the reason for the award of the King's Commendation for Valuable Service in the Air, which he received on 1 January 1949. Oxspring gave him an 'Above Average' assessment for his flying and air gunnery, and by November 1948 he had completed 1,500 hours in the air.

Frank left 54 Squadron in January 1949, and was promoted to squadron leader in July, after completing a course at the Empire Flying School, Hullavington. He took command of the Bomber Command Examining Flight, before moving on to an Air Ministry posting in 1951, followed by courses at the RAF Staff College and 209 Advanced Flying School, Weston Zoyland. Frank married in May 1951, and his wife Margaret presented him with two sons, Johnathan and Philip. He gained promotion to wing commander in March 1954, and was posted as Wg Cdr (Flying) to 123 Wing, RAF Wunsdorf. It was primarily as a result of his work with the wing that he was awarded the Air Force Cross in 1956. There followed three years as an instructor at the RAF Staff College before he went on a course to the RAF Flying College at Manby, Lincolnshire.

Frank met his death at Manby on 28 November 1959 in a flying accident, in a wayward quirk of fate he should have survived, but for extreme bad luck. At midday on the 28th, Canberra B2 jet bomber WH699 took off from Strubby airfield for Malta, with Frank acting as navigator. The pilot, Sqn Ldr P.H. Walker climbed to 1,500 feet when he felt himself losing control of the aircraft and ordered the other two crew members to eject. Wg Cdr C.E. Ness, sitting next to Woolley, saw his colleague eject first, clearing the aircraft cleanly at a safe height to survive the low-level bale-out. Ejecting aircrew had to operate their own parachutes, as no automatic opening mechanism was then provided. Sadly, Frank seems to have broken his right arm as he left the doomed bomber, and in the few vital seconds following the launch, the pain and shock from his injury prevented him from using his arm to pull the ripcord. His body was found in a field, with the unopened parachute still strapped in place. The other two crewmen both ejected safely. An inquest in December judged that the severe injury to his arm was the most likely cause of his untimely end, with the immediate trauma paralysing him for the critical period which meant the difference between life and death.

It is likely that Frank Woolley was marked for high command and, but for the intervention of blind chance, would doubtless, like his father before him, have achieved Air rank. His RAF career was both distinguished and dedicated, and his double DFC and AFC make him the most decorated Derbyshire fighter pilot of the post-1939 period. Frank was cremated and his ashes were brought to Ilkeston to lie with those of his family. This unconquerable fighting man, who was a DFC at nineteen and the noted son of a noted father, exemplifies the finest traditions of the military family *par excellence.*

Bibliography

Barker, Ralph, The Hurricats (Pelham, 1978)

Bartley, Anthony, Smoke Trails In The Sky (William Kimber, 1984)

Clostermann, Pierre, The Big Show (Chatto & Windus, 1951)

Crook, David, Spitfire Pilot (Faber & Faber, 1942)

Cull, Brian, and Bruce Lander and Heinrich Weiss, Twelve Days In May (Grub Street Publications, 1999)

Cull, Brian, and Nicola Malizia and Fredrick Galea, Spitfires Over Sicily (Grub Street Publications, 2000)

Drake, Billy, Billy Drake, Fighter Leader (Grub Street Publications, 2002)

Dundas, Hugh, Flying Start (Stanley Paul, 1988)

Franks, Norman, The Air Battle Of Dunkirk (Grub Street Publications, 2000)

Goss, Chris, Brothers In Arms (Crecy, 1994)

Holmes, Ray, Sky Spy (Airlife, 1989)

Jefford, Geoffrey, RAF Squadrons (Airlife, 1988)

Knight, Dennis, Harvest Of Messerschmitts (Warne, 1981)

Marsden, Barry M., A Few Of The Derbyshire 'Few' (KM, 1987)

—, Winged Warriors (Ryestone, 2003)

Mason, Francis K., Battle Over Britain (Aston, 1990)

Morgan, Eric, Spitfire – The History (Key, 1987)

Shacklady, Edward, and Alfred Price, The Hardest Day (Macdonald and Janes, 1979)

Ramsay, Winston G. (ed.), The Battle Of Britain – Then And Now (After The Battle, 1982)

—, The Blitz – Then And Now Vol.1 (After The Battle, 1986)

—, The Blitz – Then And Now Vol.2 (After The Battle, 1988)

Rawlings, John, Fighter Squadrons Of The RAF (Macdonald, 1969)

Rayner, Geoff, One Hurricane, One Raid (Airlife, 1990)

Richey, Paul, Fighter Pilot (Cassell, 2001)

Rolls, William T., Spitfire Attack (William Kimber, 1987)

Shaw, Michael, No.1 Squadron (Ian Allen, 1986)

Shores, Christopher, and Hans Ring, Fighters Over The Desert (Spearman, 1969)

Shores, Christopher, 2nd Tactical Air Force (Osprey, 1970)

Shores, Christopher, and Hans Ring and William N. Hess, Fighters Over Tunisia (Spearman, 1975)

Shores, Christopher, Fledgling Eagles (Grub Street, 1991)

Shores, Christopher, and Clive Williams, Aces High (Grub Street Publications, 1994)

Shores, Christopher, Dust Clouds In The Middle East (Grub Street Publications, 1996)

Wallace, Graham, RAF Biggin Hill (Tandem, 1975)

Ziegler, Frank, Under The White Rose – The Story Of 609 Squadron (Macdonald, 1971)

Other local titles published by Tempus

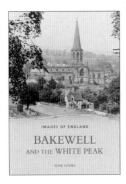

Bakewell and the White Peak
PETER TUFFREY

A stunning collection of images from the camera of Edgar Leonard Scrivens, a leading exponent of the picture postcard in Derbyshire, North Nottinghamshire and South Yorkshire. His pictures show local views prior to industrial and commercial developments, including timeless vistas of well-known landmarks including Mam Tor at Castleton and Toad Mouth Rock at Hathersage.

0 7524 3042 4

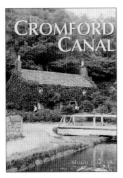

The Cromford Canal
HUGH POTTER

The Cromford Canal was a bold undertaking, linking the Derwent and Upper Erewash valleys to the main canal system of England. Collieries, ironworks, mills, limestone and gritstone quarries all flourished alongside it, and the canal passes through spectacular scenery as it contours along the steep side of the Derwent valley.

0 7524 2802 0

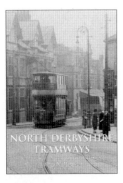

North Derbyshire Tramways
Chesterfield, Matlock and Glossop
BARRY M. MARSDEN

In the heyday of trams, no fewer than seven systems operated in Derbyshire, built at a time when tramway systems were the easiest and cheapest form of public transport. *North Derbyshire Tramways* captures the halcyon days of tramways in Chesterfield, Matlock and Glossop.

0 7524 2398 3

Prehistory in the Peak
MARK EDMONDS

Fifty years ago the Peak District was established as the first National Park in Britain. Through text and photographs, *Prehistory in the Peak* allows the reader to follow the changing character of the region over time; the ways that different landscapes were inhabited and how the pattern of people's lives helped shape the social institutions that they recognised.

0 7524 1483 6

If you are interested in purchasing other books published by Tempus, or in case you have difficulty finding any Tempus books in your local bookshop, you can also place orders directly through our website

www.tempus-publishing.com

or from   **BOOKPOST**, Freepost, PO Box 29, Douglas, Isle of Man, IM99 1BQ
tel 01624 836000   email bookshop@enterprise.net